THE BACKYARD ARCHERY PROJECT
VOLUME I

THE
IMPOSSIBLE
BOW

BUILDING ARCHERY BOWS WITH PVC PIPE

NICHOLAS TOMIHAMA

LD

Published by Levi Dream, 2011

Levi Dream Publishing, P.O. Box 75203, Honolulu, HI 96836-0203

Printed in the U.S.A., Charleston, SC

First Printing in 2011

Copyright © 2011 Nicholas Tomihama

This book is intended as an informational guide. The views expressed within are solely the opinions of the author, based on personal experience. All instructions within this book must be followed with caution, and the author, publisher, printer, and all other parties involved deny any responsibility for injury to both body and/or property due to the misuse of information contained herein.

ISBN: 978-0-9832481-5-6

NICHOLAS TOMIHAMA

TABLE OF CONTENTS

Chapter Two - Bent PVC Pipe Bows
- 31 -

The most basic of PVC bows, these are simply straight pieces of pipe that have been bent into a basic shape. They all work in the same way, and despite being able to hit high weights, are very undesirable as bows, but they are quick to make and can be fun to shoot.

NICHOLAS TOMIHAMA

CHAPTER THREE - BANDED KRAIT
- 98 -

THE BANDED KRAIT IS AN ALL-PVC BOW THAT IS FULLY-TILLERED AND SMOOTH-DRAWING. IT IS CAPABLE OF WEIGHTS UP TO SIXTY POUNDS, AND WITH A LITTLE TUNING IT CAN BE A QUIET, POWERFUL, AND COMPACT BOW FOR FISHING, HUNTING, AND TARGET SHOOTING.

CHAPTER FOUR - INDIGO SERPENT
- 126 -

MODELED AFTER THE SHORT COMPOSITE BOWS OF MONGOLIA, THE INDIGO SERPENT IS A SMALL BOW CAPABLE OF DRAWS UP TO THIRTY-TWO INCHES AND FORTY POUNDS OF PULL. IT IS NOT AN ALL PVC BOW, USING WOOD AND STRONG CORD FOR THE SIYAHS (BOW TIPS) AND STRING BRIDGES (STRING RESTS).

THE IMPOSSIBLE BOW

CHAPTER FIVE - EXTRA EQUIPMENT
- 206 -

This chapter goes over making two simple quivers, a thumb ring for the Mongolian draw, and a simple target for backyard shooting.

CHAPTER SIX - USING AND CARING FOR YOUR BOW
- 248 -

Once you've built your bow, this chapter will show you how to string it safely, how to draw the bow with your thumb, as well as tips on prolonging the life of your PVC bow and signs that tell you when to retire your bow and make a new one.

Nicholas Tomihama

INTRODUCTION -
BACKYARD ARCHERY AND PVC

When I was a kid, I always wanted a bow. I always dreamed of being Robin Hood, stealing from the rich and giving to the poor, with my bow and arrows at me side. Like most kids, I liked making my own toys out of whatever I had handy. One of my first bows was a 1/2 inch PVC pipe that was taller than I was, with a mason twine string.

Years later, I had the idea of making another bow out of PVC pipe, which was similar to my first. This was, of course, before I started building bows, and I naturally didn't know a thing about making them. It was a fun little stick flinger, but it just didn't feel or look right. Then once I started making bows, I found myself taking people to the archery range with me on the weekends.

My passion for archery was contagious, and soon I had others interested. Now I try to be generous, but I'm also practical. I had friends who wanted bows for shooting in their backyards or at archery ranges that were in their areas, but didn't have the money or time to make or buy bows for them all. That's when I got thinking about and experimenting with PVC, trying to make something remotely bow-like that I could just give away to those interested in archery.

The bows in the first chapter on bows come from that original idea of a quick and easy bow. Then when my first book, The Backyard Bowyer was finally published, I started getting more interested in what PVC could do if worked properly. I've used it in a variety of ways, but the easiest way to make a bow with PVC is to just work with PVC pipe in its whole form.

While the first bows in this book are in no way efficient bows, the last two come close. This book is a culmination of what I have learned, to allow others who otherwise could not get involved with archery due to expense to join the ever-growing family of archers and bowyers. Hopefully the thrill of being able to plant an arrow into a mark 40 yards off with nothing but a bent piece of plumbing pipe will kindle the fire of traditional archery like it has for me.

There seems to be, now more than ever, a large number of people who shoot bows in their backyard. It's not new, but I see more and more people trying to start archery at home, either on the lawn or down the hallway. There are people making their own bows and arrows out of everything imaginable, sometimes very dangerously. Yet there is a spirit to it that cannot be denied, and hopefully I can serve as a guide to those who wish to go that route as safely as possible.

I am a bowyer, and no self-respecting bowyer I know would ever take a PVC bow seriously. That said, these bows are in no way meant to match or even come close to a well made bow. They barely fit into the bow-like-object category, but they do work, they are not expensive, and they can be a lot of fun if you let them.

These bows, like "proper bows" (still haven't figured out what that really means), can be dangerous. They should never be aimed at people, pets, or objects that could be damaged. They are considered weapons, and can even bring down game in some cases (check your local laws). These are not toys, and should not be treated as such. They may be slow and awkward compared to modern bows, but they can stand toe-to-toe with many of the early bows that have sustained man for eons.

With that said, let's get started!

CHAPTER ONE –
GETTING STARTED

Before we get started making some bows, take a look through this section. Here you'll find a little primer on how to select good PVC pipe, what the different designations on plastic pipe mean, and how to check that your PVC pipe is safe for making bows. We'll also go over how to heat and bend with heat and how to cut PVC without a saw or pipe cutter if you ever needed to.

This chapter will also go over some basic tools that you want to have to get started. Don't worry, if you don't have some of these, you can go without. All you really need is a heat source and some patience for these bows. And finally, we'll go over safety and precautions when dealing with PVC pipe, dust, and fumes.

We'll start with selecting PVC pipe.

SELECTING PIPE

The first part to making a good PVC bow is find good pipe to start out with. Certain types of PVC pipe work better than others, and there are many varieties of pipe out there. There are different sizes, thicknesses, and even plastic compositions. Sometimes plastic pipe that has been stored outdoors or exposed to temperature extremes may become brittle and unsuitable for making bows. Ultimately, everything comes down to the quality of pipe you use.

FINDING GOOD PIPE

The best type of pipe to use is new pipe that has been stored properly. Most hardware and home improvement stores carry PVC pipe and keep it in good condition. When buying new pipe, make sure you pick from the newest dates, as most pipe will be marked with at least the year of manufacture somewhere along the pipe. The pipe should also be white if it is of the white variety and gray if of the gray variety. Yellow or brown pipe should be avoided as it may be brittle or unsafe to use in a bow.

If you plan on using found pipe, make sure it is not currently in use. Taking apart existing water lines or electrical wiring is always risky and I don't suggest it. If there has been pipe lying around outside, it is probably too brittle. If you hit it with a hammer with reasonable force, good pipe won't crack. Bad pipe could shatter, and it's a good test of whether the pipe is okay to use. If you've got some pipe that's been sitting in a basement for a while and it's only a few years old, it should be fine.

SCHEDULE AND DIAMETER

In the book, I will be referring to pipe by schedule and diameter. Schedule is a method of standardizing pipe size. The most common schedules are 20, 40, and 80. These numbers refer to the wall thicknesses of the pipe, so schedule 20 is thinner than 40, which is thinner than 80. Schedule 40 is the most common pipe, and the one carried by most hardware stores. For bows, I would suggest sticking to schedule 40, but if you like the way a bow feels in size, but want it lighter or heavier, the other schedules can help you do that.

Diameter, or inside diameter (ID), is basically a standardized measurement of the inside of the pipe. This ensures that all pipes of one size are compatible and have the same capacity. The common sizes are 1/2", 3/4", 1", and 1 1/4". These pipes may seem misleading, because the measurement is much smaller than the outside of the pipe. For example, 3/4" pipe is actually closer to 1" in diameter.

Schedule and diameter are both printed on the outside of the pipe, along the side. The diameter may be labeled I.D., or simply have the number. The schedule is usually marked with schedule or SCHED or it may simply have a number. If your pipe is unmarked or you have a section that only has other information, you can find the schedule and diameter by measuring the pipe. To find the diameter, simply measure the inside of the pipe across. The diameter should come close to one of the set diameters. If it doesn't you may have another type of pipe. To find schedule, measure the wall thickness. For schedule 40, the thickness is around 1/8".

There is also another method of standardizing pipe called SDR. In SDR, pipes are organized in terms of pressure rating, not wall thicknesses, as the larger the pipe, the thicker the walls need to be to maintain the same pressure rating. Pipes that say SDR or have a strange number like 21 are usually of this type. They are usually very thin and easily collapse, so are not suitable for most bows.

PLUMBING PIPE VS ELECTRICAL CONDUIT

To further confuse you, one final thing to consider is whether to use plumbing pipe or electrical conduit for your bows. There are advantages to both, and both have their strengths and weaknesses. Both will work for these bows, and some designs do better with one or the other. Though, ultimately, it all comes down to your own preferences.

Plumbing pipe is usually white, though it can sometimes be

gray. Gray pipe is usually made for outdoor plumbing applications, and if you can find it, it is better than electrical conduit, but still has some of its downfalls. White plumbing pipe is rigid and can be brittle. It is very dense and made to withstand high pressure and pressure cycles that occur with water piping. As a result, this pipe can hold up to use and does not fatigue too quickly. The downside is that it is brittle, so the possibility of breakage is high and it is affected by sunlight, which can easily weaken it. When it breaks, the shards are usually very sharp and can cut.

Electrical conduit is gray and has added ingredients that make it more flexible and resistant to breakage than plumbing pipe. It also has UV stabilizers that make it resistant to sunlight and therefore make it a lower-maintenance bow. It is not designed to hold under pressure, so it can be softer. This makes it less able to spring back after each shot, so bows made of conduit are usually of a lower weight and are more prone to taking an extreme permanent bend than plumbing pipe. The plus side is that these bows can hold up to more abuse and don't need as much maintenance as plumbing pipe bows. It also shatters when it breaks, but the shards are usually not that sharp, the edges coming out more crumbly and rounded.

Basically, there are a couple trade-offs that will decide which pipe you will go with for your bow. First, the possibility of violent bow failure. Plumbing pipe, because it resists bending more and is more brittle, is more prone to shattering, though if it is cared for properly this is not a real problem. Next, there is maintenance and upkeep. For this, electrical conduit wins again, as it can be left out in the sun longer and can be tossed around and bumped around with less effect than plumbing pipe. These make conduit the choice for safety and if the bow is going to be used by kids or in adverse conditions.

The banded krait styles bows, made with conduit and at seventy pounds, are my preferred PVC hunting bows in dense jungle or dense foliage. The conduit makes them take huge amounts of set, and they are quite sluggish in the shot, though the power is there. I like them because I can keep one in the car at all times, and they are so short and maneuverable (just as short and much lighter than my compound) that they make great bows for that purpose.

Plumbing pipe makes a bow that is more fragile (not any more fragile than a laminated fiberglass bow) but with higher performance (not as much performance as a laminated fiberglass bow). When it comes to arrow speed, plumbing pipe drives an arrow just a little faster than conduit. The bow also keeps its shape better, allowing for better performance. Plumbing pipe also fatigues slower and less than conduit, so the overall life of the bow is much higher if the bow is cared for well.

In the gallery near the end of the book you will find two bows made in the banded krait style, but much longer. These bows, starting with five foot plus pipe, are very good target bows, and have the speed and power of similar solid fiberglass bows. At a little under five feet long and fifty pounds, a plumbing pipe bow becomes a formidable hunting weapon. These are my favorite bows for open fields or areas without a lot of dense growth. At fifty pounds, these bows work just as well as the seventy pound bows, but they are much longer and must be cared for a little more.

So if you want more performance, go with plumbing pipe. If you want more safety and the ability to really toss the bow around, conduit is your material of choice.

BENDING WITH HEAT AND BREAKING

PVC pipe is very easy to work with and has a lot of properties that make it a near effortless material to cut, shape, and bend. PVC is a thermoplastic, which means it is basically like glass. It has a molecular structure much like a fluid, and lacks a tight crystalline structure. This makes it somewhat brittle when cool, but this unique structure keeps it from being affected from heating up and cooling down, as the structure does not change like in a crystalline solid. This means that it can be heated up, reshaped, and then cooled and still retain all its original properties.

Like glass, PVC can be bent and shaped with heat. Heating and re-forming PVC is what this book is all about, and is the backbone of all the bows in the book. Like glass, PVC can also be cut through scoring and breaking. This allows you to cut lengths of pipe without the use of a saw or pipe-cutter.

Bending Pipe

Bending and flattening pipe is the basis for this whole book, and is the main technique used to manipulate the PVC pipe into a bow-like shape. Bending pipe is quite simple to do and only requires a few things. First, you need a heat source. The easiest heat source to work with is a gas range. Electric ranges, burners, grills, and even open fires all work. Torches work as well, but you have to really be careful not to burn the pipe. If you have one, a heat gun is probably the best to use as it gives nice even heat without burning the pipe easily.

Second, you need a flat surface to work on. This surface will be the one on which your bow will rest on while it is soft, so it will conform to any dips, shifts, or uneven surfaces. If you wanted to, your could build jigs for flattening, but bending round pipe with a jig can be problematic unless the pipe is under pressure, which can be tricky without some expensive equipment. You also need something like an oven mitt or heat-resistant glove to handle the pipe, as it gets very hot when soft. Last of all, you should have a source of water nearby to cool down and rapidly solidify any bends or flattened limbs. This isn't necessary, but requires a good deal of patience for the pipe to air-cool.

THE IMPOSSIBLE BOW

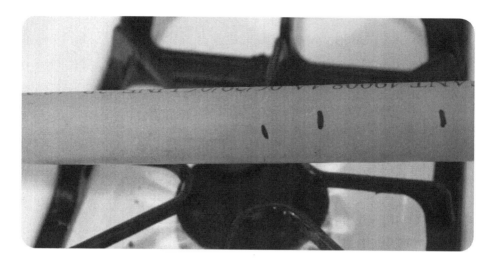

Move the pipe over your heat source, careful not to get too close. If the pipe starts turning yellow at all, you are too close.

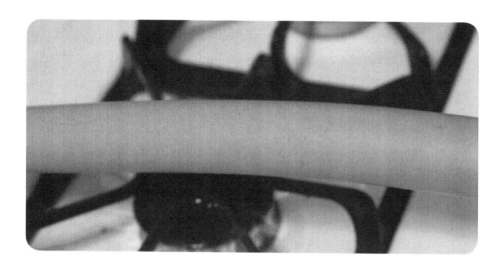

It may take a while, but eventually the pipe will begin to droop slightly. Move on to a different section or pull it off the heat for a few seconds.

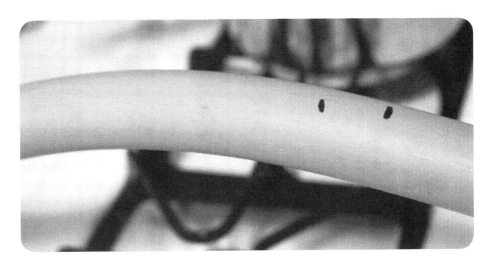

Bring it back over the heat, a little farther away, continually moving and turning it over until the pipe is very elastic. Now it can be bent, shaped, flattened, and formed with ease.

BREAKING PIPE

If you do not have a chop saw but want to make nice, clean cuts in PVC you can score and break the pipe, similarly to cutting glass. All you need to cut PVC pipe in this way is a knife and an edge, like the edge of a table or a step to break the pipe on. This method can also be used to cut pipe with stone if you ever find yourself needing to cut PVC pipe out in the middle of nowhere (but how, I ask, would you even have plastic pipe in such a situation).

THE IMPOSSIBLE BOW

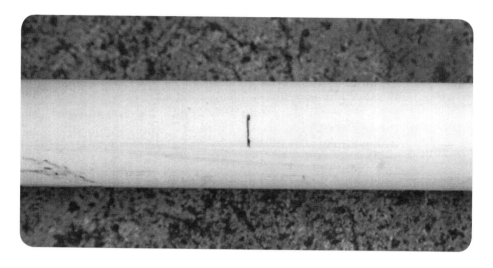

Start by marking the area you want to cut.

With a knife, cut a thin line going all the way around the pipe, going lightly and simply making a shallow mark.

Here's the shallow line. Make sure it is even, or how you want the pipe to break.

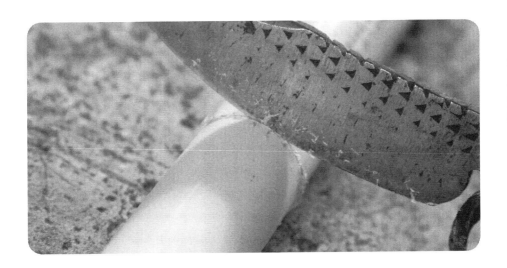

Go back and now deepen the lines. Your cut should be about halfway into the pipe's thickness, which is not that deep.

THE IMPOSSIBLE BOW

Find a sharp edge or a rounded edge, and then holding both sides of the line, strike the cut line hard against the edge.

Now you have a nice clean break where your line was.

TOOLS

While there are few tools you absolutely need for making PVC bows, there are a variety of tools which can come in handy. Most of these tools can be found cheaply, and many of them can be substituted for others. All you really need for making these bows is a flat area, something to cut the pipe to length, a heat source, something to cut nocks, a string, and some arrows. You could do everything with a knife, but it does help to have some of these other tools as well.

SAWS

A good saw really helps save time when cutting pipe down to size, as well as shaping and cutting nocks. There are many saws you can use. There are saws just for plastic, but any saw for cutting wood will work for plastic as well. I like to have either a chop saw or a larger saw for cutting pieces as I get a straight cut. For smaller cuts a hacksaw or a coping saw comes in handy.

FILES

A small set of files can make any finish shaping work a breeze. Whether cutting nocks, smoothing rough edges, or shaping wood for

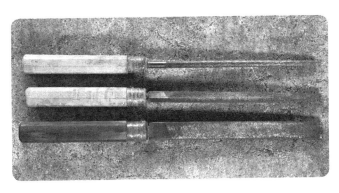

use in siyahs and string bridges, a good set of files is indispensable.

The Impossible Bow

I like to have a flat, round, and triangle 8-10 inch files, and round, flat, and half round needle files. The needle files come in handy for smoothing out any small areas.

Sandpaper

Sandpaper is good for cleaning up the ends of pipe and for smoothing any rough spots. There are many different types of sandpaper available, but in most cases, you only need a few grits, mostly from about sixty to four hundred.

Tape

When building wood bows, I like to use leather and natural fibers. When making PVC bows, I like using tape.

There are a variety of tapes that can be used for decoration, added comfort, and added safety. Duct tape, electrical tape, and fiberglass strapping tape are all important tapes to have on hand.

Tiller

A tiller is not something that is 100% needed for PVC bows. A tiller is used for checking the bend of a bow while it is being made, but these bows usually don't require that. While a tiller can help in fine-tuning a bow and measuring draw weight, most of the

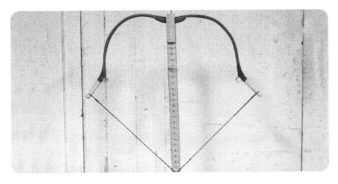

time just looking at the bow or having someone else draw it is enough.

Strings

Without a string, a bow is useless, so strings are pretty important. I always advocate buying a good Dacron string from an archery pro shop, or from online, but I realize that a book on PVC bows would be in sad shape if the most important part of the bow was thrown to the wayside like that. Really, any really strong rope will do. 550 paracord, the good stuff (military spec, 7 strands of twisted nylon, woven nylon shell), makes a good string for bows even up to one hundred pounds or more. Nylon is stretchy, but really, these are PVC bows. Not much more needs to be said. If you want to see a good knot for stringing up a bow with rope, go the Ye Olde String Flinger chapter at the back of the book.

If you decide to buy or make a string, make sure it is the right length for your bow. To figure out the proper length, measure the bow's length from tip to tip and subtract about four to five inches. There are two main types of string, continuous loop and a twisted string. The twisted style of string is often called a Flemish string. Both work well, and both have reasonably long life expectancies if taken care of. Make sure that these strings get rubbed down with string or bee's wax

THE IMPOSSIBLE BOW

periodically, and the servings (wrappings on the string where the arrow rests and where the loops are) are not coming apart.

There are lots of materials for strings, but for the bows in this book, the older synthetics like Dacron and polyester work fine. If you plan on making your own strings, Dacron fishing line, heavy Dacron thread, bookbinding linen, and quality hemp can all make good strings. The best string in my opinion has one loop on one end, and the other end is secured with a knot like the one shown in the very back of the book. This enables the string to be shortened or lengthened as needed, and the string can be used for multiple bows.

ARROWS

I have heard many people boast about their bows and their equipment, how well tuned it all is and how everything is perfect. Then, when they lose their set of four matched arrows, their equipment becomes almost useless. It's pretty sad when I can stand toe to toe with a modern recurve bow flinging carbon arrows with a PVC pipe and wooden sticks. Arrows are pretty important, and as is my custom, I recommend you buy some arrows. Even if you want to make your own, buy a couple arrows so you can get a feel for what they look like and how they work.

Resist the temptation to run to the craft or hardware store, get some dowels, and start shooting a fifty pound bow. Not a good combination. Dowels are great if you know how to use them. If you really want to make your own arrows, I have another book, The Dowel Arrow Handbook, that shows how to make them. If

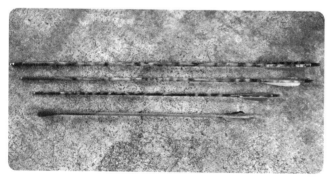

you want to make other types of arrows, that's a whole nother can of worms. I think making good bows is easier than making good arrows.

There

26

Tools

are lots of types of arrows out there. If buying arrows, there are a few choices to make. There are arrows made of wood, aluminum, fiberglass, and carbon or graphite. Wood is my personal favorite, just make sure the arrows you get are strong enough for use in your bow, as many wood arrows sold are just for kids and low weight bows. Aluminum arrows are great for everything, are pretty hard to break, and are very accurate. These are my favorite to recommend to others, but I personally love wood arrows. Fiberglass arrows are usually just for lightweight youth bows, and are prone to splintering. Carbon fiber and graphite arrows are the latest in performance arrows. These are great for compounds, recurves with arrow rests, and longbows with rests. If shooting of the hand, like the bows in this book, avoid carbon as it has a pesky habit of either splintering without warning, or shedding carbon fibers into your shooting hand.

If trying to get kids into shooting, invest in some good wood or aluminum arrows. They aren't that expensive, especially for the lighter weights. Thirty dollars a dozen is not hard to find for lighter arrows, (compare that to upwards of sixty dollars a dozen for higher weights, or more than fifteen dollars an arrow for the really high-tech sharpened sticks). There are also blunt and padded arrows used for LARP and medieval combat that make good arrows for kids to shoot in the yard. These can be made fairly easily with tape and foam rubber.

Heat Source

Another thing you need to make PVC bows is a heat source. Most of the bows in this book are made by forming, flattening, or shaping PVC,  and in order to do that, the plastic needs to be made soft. Heat is the easiest way to do this. What you want is nice even heat that

THE IMPOSSIBLE BOW

is somewhat spread out, like a stovetop. Like I said before, a gas range or heat gun works the best, but any cook top or hot pate, torch, or even camp stove works. Even an open fire or grill can work if you are careful.

OTHER TOOLS

Other tools like the power varieties of saws and sandpaper (chop saw, band saw, jigsaw, scroll saw, belt sander, disc sander, etc.) can also be used, just be sure to wear adequate respiratory and eye protection. You can also use a specialized pipe cutter for cutting PVC pipe. Other things you should have include a pen or pencil for marking and a measuring device of some sort.

SAFETY

Safety is incredibly important when doing anything. You can always make more stuff, but you can't make a new you (this still holds true, and I don't see that changing any time soon). Your hands, eyes, lungs, and the rest of your body are important and cannot be easily fixed or replaced if anything happens to them. There are a variety of safety issues that come with working with PVC as a material. Bows are dangerous in their own right, and the ones in the book are capable of causing major injury or death if they are misused. There are a few major topics on safety we'll cover here.

HEATING AND CUTTING PVC

PVC plastic is fairly stable, and there are few things that make it unsafe. Yet, this plastic can release a few chemicals, especially chlorine, that can cause damage if inhaled or if it comes in contact with skin. When heated, PVC can release fumes, which make being in a well-ventilated area a must. While gentle heating is no problem, burning can cause a great deal of fumes to be released. If you can smell the pipe burning, make sure to get out of the area, as this can have detrimental effects on your health. Also make sure to wear heat resistant gloves when working with hot PVC as it can cause burns and melt onto skin, causing prolonged, severe burns.

When cutting PVC with a saw or using sandpaper (especially if using power tools), the dust and fumes released can be harmful. Always wear proper lung protection when sanding or cutting PVC. A respirator and face mask or shield are great to wear, and it also helps to be in a well-ventilated or open area. The benefit of making bows with PVC is that everything can be done with minimal power tools, and almost all work can be done outdoors. Also be careful as anything that can cut PVC can cut you. Wear gloves and always be mindful of your work.

PVC as a Bow Material

As resilient PVC is as a plastic, it was not designed to be used as a bow material. While it has many properties that make it suitable for making bows, just using PVC brings up many inherent risks. Because PVC pipe is not manufactured for making bows, there can be inconsistencies in the material that would not compromise its use as pipe, but may prove devastating if used in a bow. Because PVC is extruded, there may be spots that are brittle or weak that may snap or collapse if flexed like a bow. That said, PVC can be an excellent material for bows if it is cared for.

PVC pipes, and most tubular construction bows, can collapse. A tube gains a great deal of its strength from its tubular shape. If strain in one spot becomes too much for the tube to bear, it may collapse, which suddenly causes the strength in that area to drop. This in itself is not a big problem, as most of the time a collapse will simply cause a bow to bend hard in that area and not break apart.

If the temperature is low enough or the PVC brittle enough, a collapse could also be accompanied by PVC shattering. Because PVC is essentially like a glass, it can produce razor sharp shards which can cut, and the broken limbs can also strike the user or people nearby, causing injury. This is a problem that can befall any bow, but is especially true of PVC. Make sure to exercise caution any time a PVC bow is used to avoid collapse or bow explosions.

The Impossible Bow

Bow Safety

Finally, these PVC bows are just that, bows. From the very beginning of man's relationship to the bow, it has been a tool for survival, a companion in all situations, and a weapon. All bows should be regarded as such, and can be dangerous and deadly if they are taken lightly. Never point a bow at another person, whether there is an arrow on the bow or not. While most of these bows should not be used for hunting, they still have a capability to maim or kill, and should be respected for that. Never fire a bow into an area you can't see, or in the direction of houses or other people. Even if you think you are a safe distance away, a situation can always arise. It is better to be safe than to cause injury or property damage, even if it is accidental.

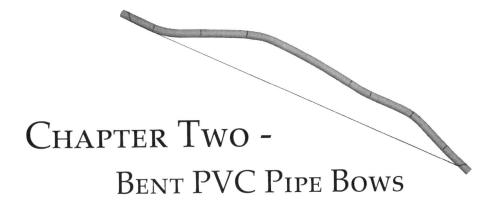

CHAPTER TWO -
BENT PVC PIPE BOWS

The most logical way to make a bow out of PVC pipe for most people is to simply take a length of pipe, put a string on it, and viola! You've got yourself a bow. PVC is amazing in its ability to flex, to hold under tension and hold against compression without breaking, and can do things that traditional bow-making materials can't.

When dealing with bows, especially those of wood, tiller is important. Tiller is basically how the bow flexes when it is drawn. A well-tillered longbow will bend evenly at almost all points along its length, creating a graceful curve. If left untillered, like a PVC pipe. Most wood would simply snap in the center due to the amazing amount of stress.

In this respect, PVC is unique in its ability to withstand these forces, but even so, this simple bow is prone to breaking, due to those forces. Most of the bows in this section have curves and bends that are applied with heat, some of them bringing the bow to its strung-up profile. The reason behind this is to give the pipe as much flex in the right areas as possible to lessen the amount of stress the pipe is under.

For this reason these bows are usually very loose when strung, don't pull very heavy for most of the draw, then harden up and gain weight right before the end of the draw. The advantage to bending the pipe beforehand is that the pipe is less likely to fold over or shatter than if the pipe remained straight.

These bows are very quick to make, and although this chapter includes measurements, only a rough approximation of the bends is required. The reason is that essentially all these bows are the same, just a PVC pipe with a string on either end, and all work about equally. These eight designs are really just to get you inspired to come up with your own designs. One thing about these bows is that they can be bent into so many shapes, that they can be made to resemble many different styles of bow from around the world, at least at a distance.

These bows are pretty versatile, and while their usefulness is really only for fun shooting, the possibility of an inexpensive, easy to make bow allows anyone interested in archery to give it a try. While these bows may register as being of a high weight (60-70 pounds is not unreasonable), they should not be used for hunting as their actual arrow speed is quite low.

While not the greatest bow, these are a nice place to start. They cost very little to make, and can take as little as ten minutes to build. They make great bows for kids, props, and other non-sporting archery.

This chapter is broken up into three sections. The first section goes over how to make short bows with a short draw, the second goes over full draw bows, and the third goes over a simple way of protecting the handle from wear and breakage.

Short Draw Bows

Ever since the earliest bows, there have always been reasons to foster the development of very, very short bows. While most bows under three feet in length were seldom drawn back further than an arm's length, some extreme bows have the capability for full draws even at this short length. As for the majority of very short bows, the draw is short as well.

These bows were built primarily to take advantage of their small size and short draw. The first bow, East Wind, roughly inspired by the short bows of Japan, was designed for the use in a palanquin. Traditionally, these were made from the tough, almost fiberglass-like baleen of whales. Lords or officials who rode in palanquin or even later when carriages were used, needed a small weapon capable of being maneuvered, drawn, and fired within the confines of these small, boxlike vehicles.

The Prairie Rattler, named for a poisonous snake of the American Plains, is a short bow reminiscent of the bows used by some native tribes of the Great Plains. This bow has a gull-wing profile and draws to almost a half-circle. Bows like this would have been of great use either on horseback or for clearing low brush, and were traditionally wood with layers of animal tendon and sinew glued onto the back.

The Seal Stalker is loosely based off of some bows used by the peoples of the northern regions of North America and Asia. These bows were short, though often because the materials at hand warranted short bows. Many bows were made of animal parts, sometimes with a wood core, sometimes just of bone and sinew. While short, they worked well enough to provide food for the people that built them. This bow also works well as the prod for medieval style crossbows, and is similar to the shape for many recurved crossbow prods.

The fourth and final bow, the Bison, is a heavier version of

THE IMPOSSIBLE BOW

the Prairie Rattler. It makes use of folded over nocks that prevent the string from slipping, and can reach up to a twenty-four inch draw. Bows similar to this style were used on horseback to bring down Bison from a very short range, sometimes even within arms reach of the animal, a testament to horse, rider, and bow.

These four bows range in draw weight from around fifteen pounds to over seventy at full draw. These bows are built off of 1/2 inch and 3/4 inch PVC pipe, the former being easier to draw, while the latter is hard to pull and stacks very hard, very fast.

If designing your own bow, just keep in mind that the ends need to either be pinched flat or hooked up, as the strings may just slip off without warning. Alternatively, you could drill your string anchors, or simply cut side nocks. While the pipe can be pulled further than twenty inches, they often collapse if pulled too far. This is much easier to do with the smaller pipe, as the thicker 3/4 inch pipe will stop bending after a certain distance, which will tell you when to stop pulling.

While I wouldn't suggest any of these bows for hunting, they make great bows for fishing in shallow water. The fact that they are all PVC allows them to be completely unaffected from being immersed in water. You can drop them in water, get them wet, and a few times I've taken them swimming with me to get to a better spot or retrieve a stuck arrow.

East Wind

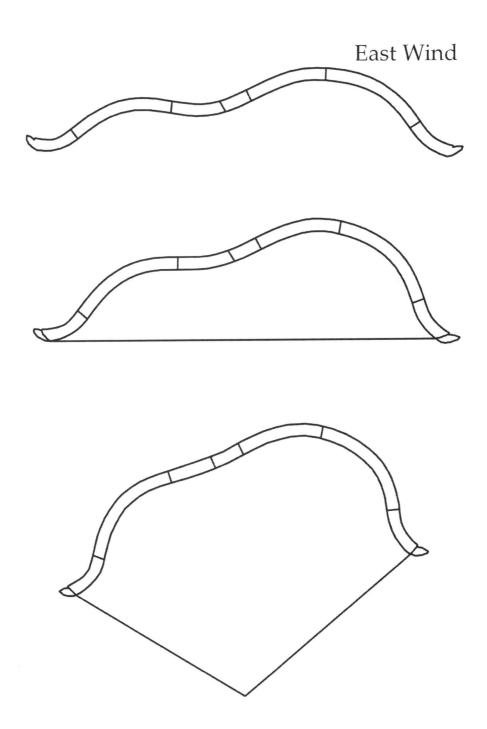

THE IMPOSSIBLE BOW

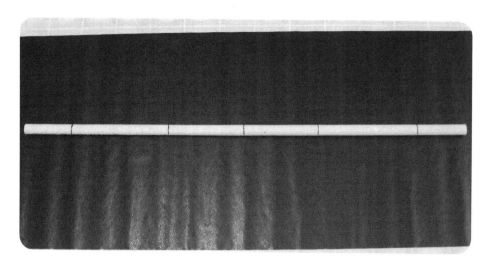

Start with a three foot section of 1/2 inch pipe. Mark the center, six inches from the center in both directions, and four inches in from both ends.

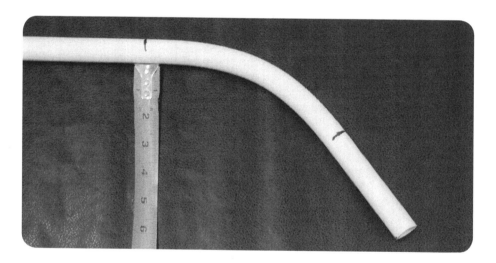

Heat the pipe between the end and mid-limb marks until it flexes easily and smoothly. With the pipe on a flat surface, bend the pipe so that the very end of the pipe rests between six and six and a half inches from the main pipe.

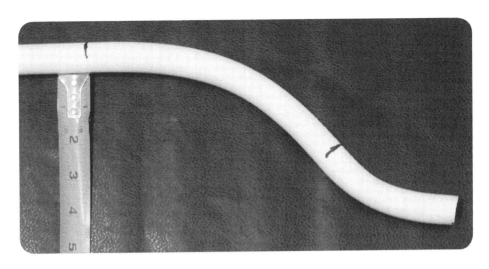

Heat the tip section of the pipe mainly near the inside section. Once it is flexible, gently bend it up towards the front of the bow. Bend it up to about four to five inches, careful not to crimp or smash the pipe.

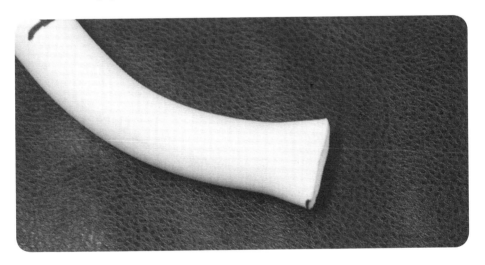

Heat the last inch of pipe and then press it together, flattening the end out.

THE IMPOSSIBLE BOW

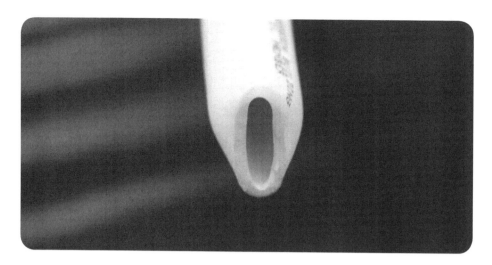

Make sure to keep the tip centered with the top and bottom edges lining up with the rest of the bow. The tip does not need to be closed, as we will be cutting it later.

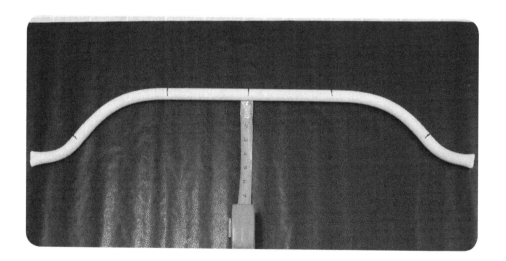

Repeat the bends to the other limb, then flip the bow over.

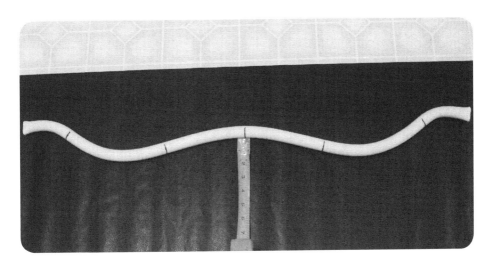

With the bow turned over so that the tips face up, heat and bend the very center of the bow. Bend it back so that the mid-limb lines come to one inch.

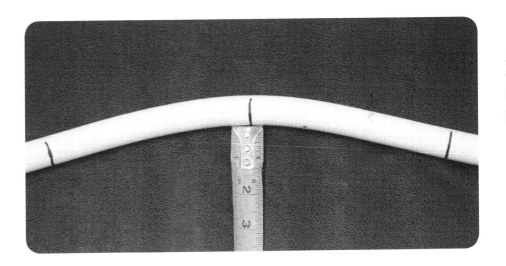

Here's a close-up so you can see the bend a little better. It should be a nice gentle bend for the first few inches around the center, not a sharp v-bend.

The Impossible Bow

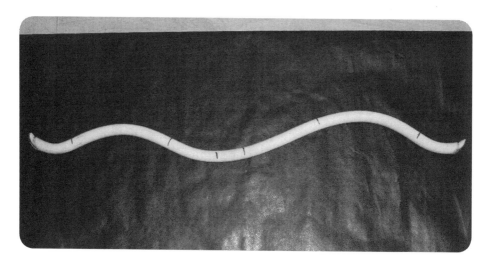

Next, mark two inches away from center on one side. Heat that area, then bend it so that one side ends up being larger, like shown.

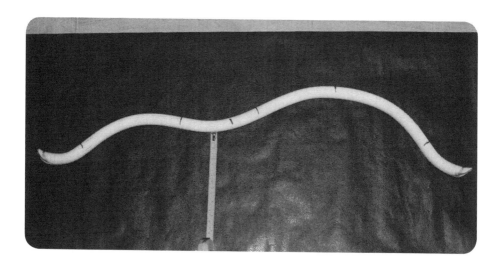

Heat the mid limb of the larger curve, then bend the limb back until the tips reach three inches.

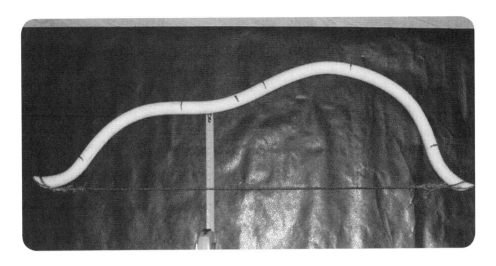

String the bow to a five inch brace.

This bow can be drawn to about twenty inches. While it certainly could be pulled further, the pipe could possibly break, or at least collapse. It's a fun little bow to shoot, and its asymmetry gives less handshock than the other designs.

The Impossible Bow

Prairie Rattler

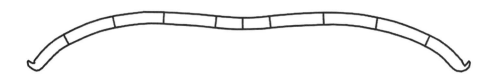

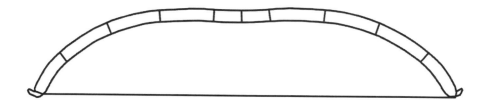

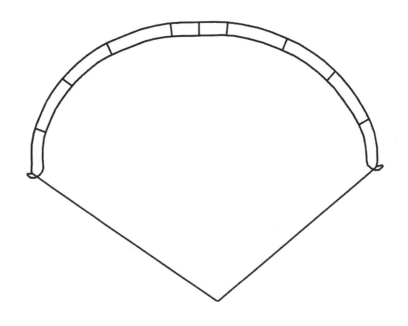

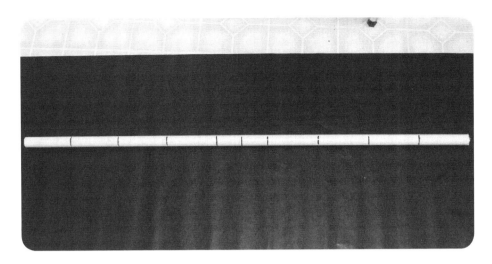

Start with a three foot length of 1/2 inch pipe. Mark four inch sections down the length of the pipe, and mark the center, cutting the center section into two, two inch sections.

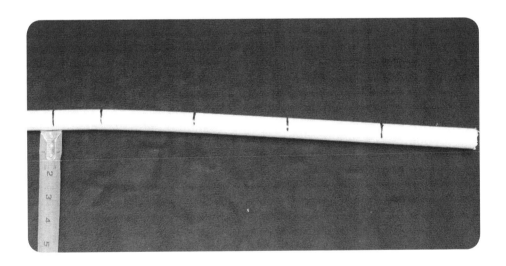

Heat the first section (right next to the handle) and bend until the tip of the pipe reaches one inch.

THE IMPOSSIBLE BOW

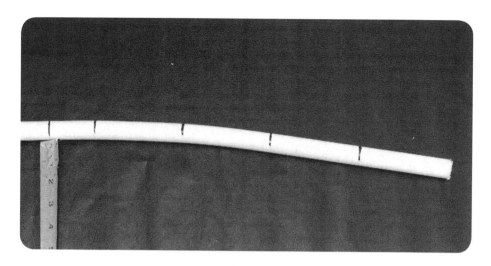

Heat and bend the second section until the tip reaches two inches.

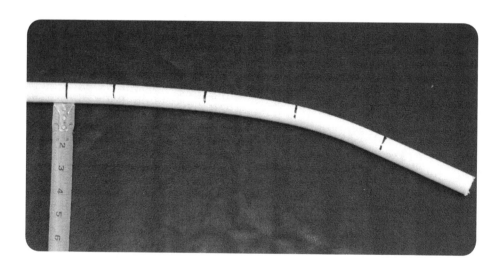

Heat and bend the third section until the tip reaches four inches.

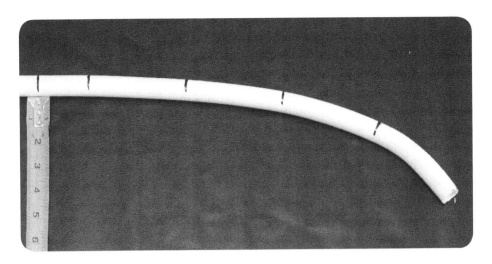

Heat and bend the end section until the tip reaches five inches.

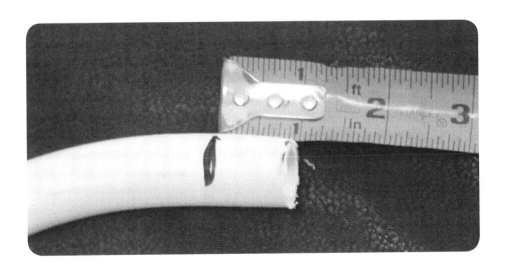

Measure one inch in from the end of the pipe.

The Impossible Bow

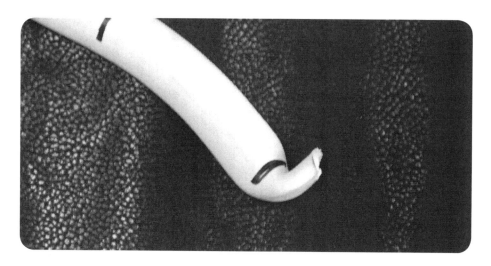

Heat the end until it is pliable, then smash it on a flat surface, causing it to bend upwards like this.

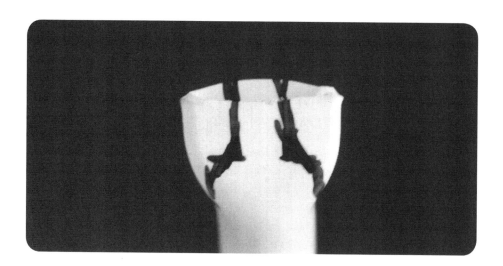

Mark and cut the end of the pipe like this, to give the string a place to sit on the bow.

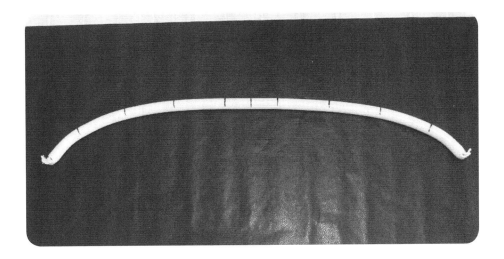

Repeat on the other limb.

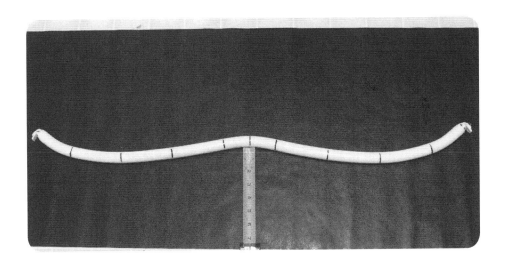

Flip the bow over and heat the handle section. Bend it back until the mid limb lines reach one inch down.

THE IMPOSSIBLE BOW

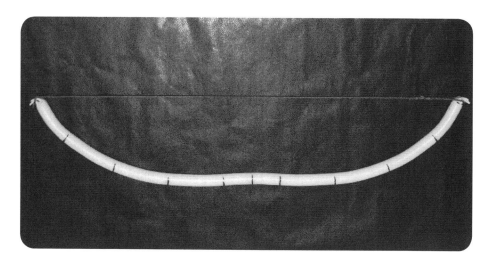

Flip the bow back over and string it up to a brace of five inches.

Here's the bow at full draw. Of all the short draw bows, this one is the easiest to shoot, and is great for kids.

Seal Stalker

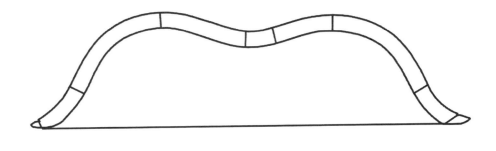

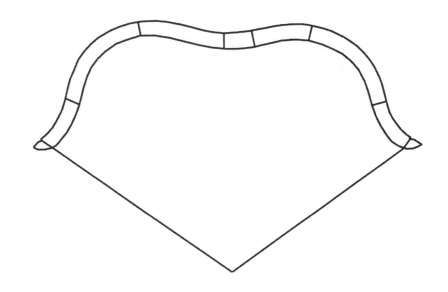

THE IMPOSSIBLE BOW

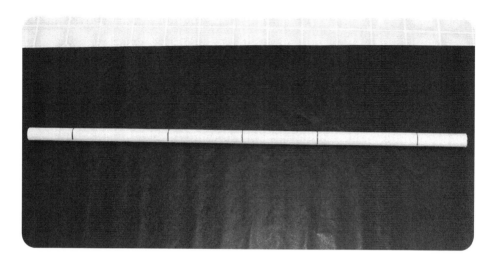

Start with a three foot section of 3/4 inch pipe. Mark the center, six inches from the center in both directions, and four inches in from both ends.

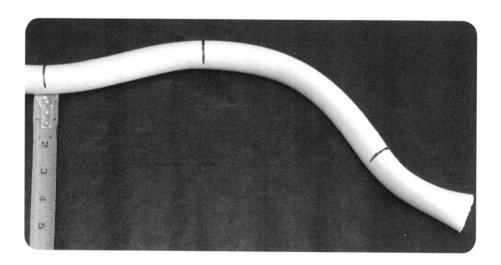

Following the first seven steps of the East Wind, heat and bend the first limb into this shape.

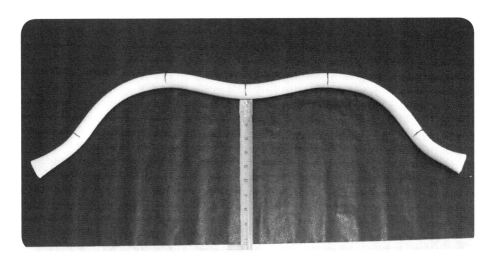

Repeat the bends on the other limb.

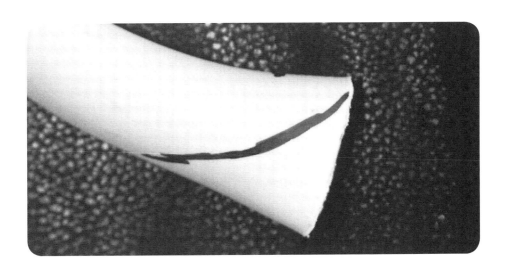

Mark a nice, curving line from the tip of the flattened tip till about where it the pipe rounds out again. Mark a place for the nock half an inch in.

THE IMPOSSIBLE BOW

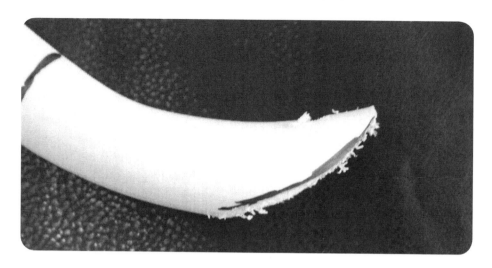

Cut the tip and nock.

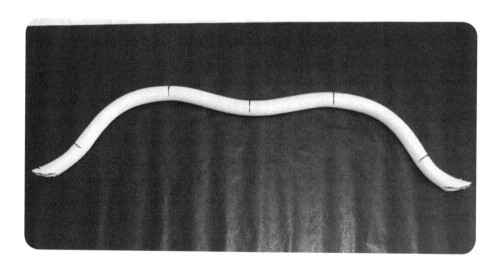

Repeat on the other tip.

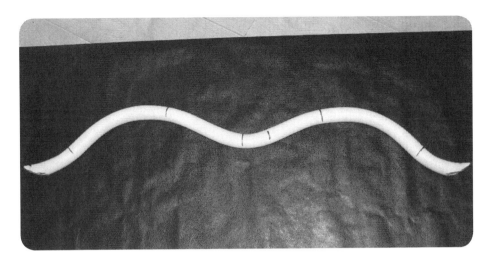

Heat and bend the center forward until the handle rests about three inches from the bottom of the tips. Mark an arrow placement two inches from the center on one side.

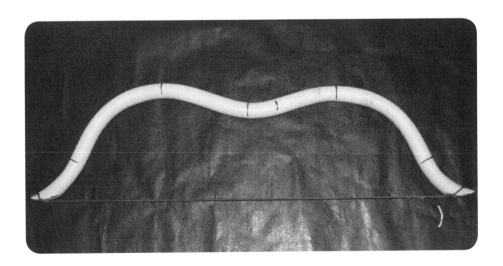

String the bow up to a brace of five inches.

THE IMPOSSIBLE BOW

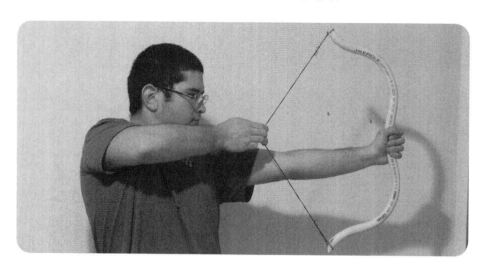

At full draw, this bow is incredibly stiff and unyielding. It would make a good crossbow prod, coming out to around sixty to seventy pounds at twenty inches.

The Bison

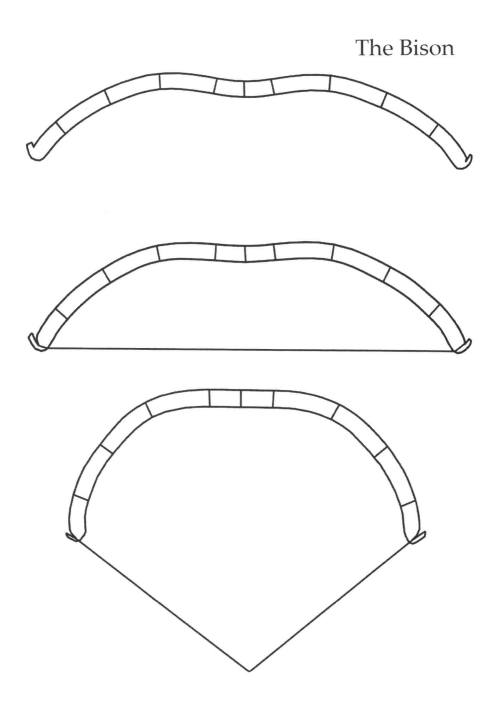

THE IMPOSSIBLE BOW

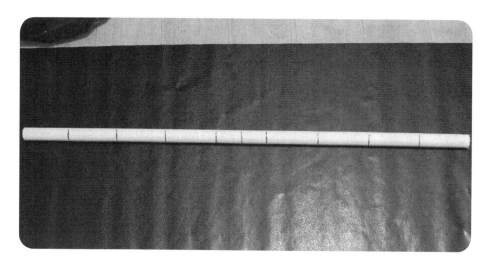

Start with a three foot length of 3/4 inch pipe. Mark four inch sections down the length of the pipe, and mark the center, separating the center section into two, two inch sections.

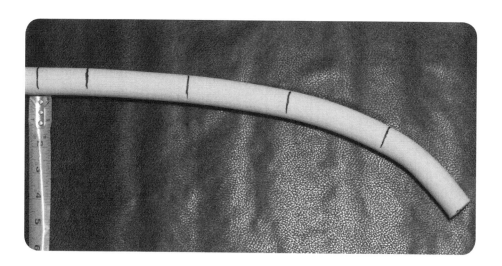

Following the first five steps of the Prairie Rattler, heat and bend one limb until it reaches back to five inches.

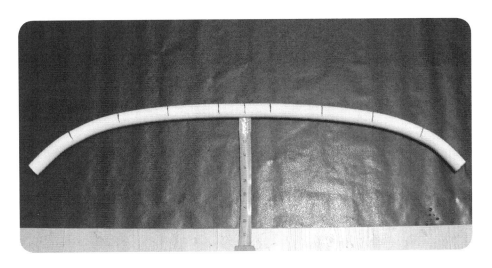

Repeat on the other limb.

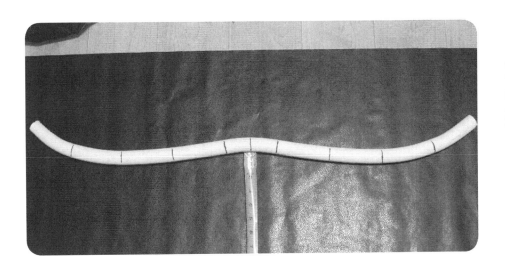

Flip the bow over. Heat and bend the handle until the mid limb marks of both limbs reach down one inch.

THE IMPOSSIBLE BOW

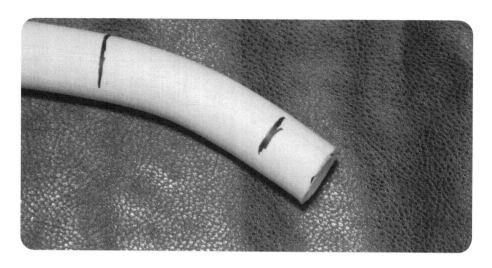

Measure in one inch from the end of the pipe.

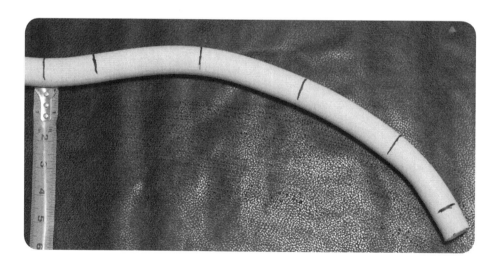

Heat and bend the inner limb line, the line closest to the handle section, till the end of the pipe reaches six inches.

The Bison

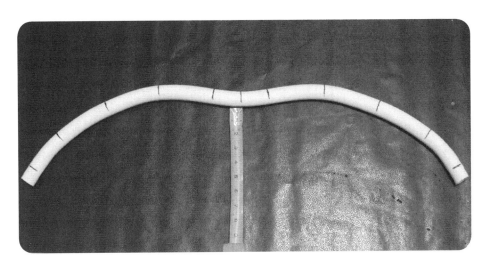

Repeat on the other limb.

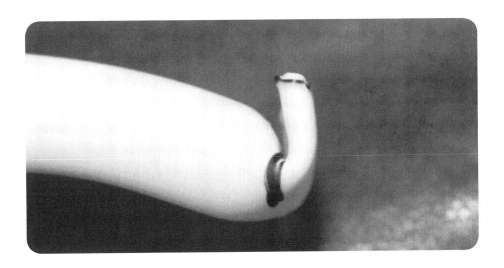

Heat the tip of the pipe from the end to the one inch mark. Press the tip flat against a smooth surface, smashing it upwards like this.

THE IMPOSSIBLE BOW

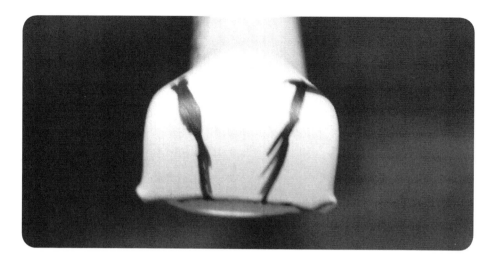

Cut the tip of the pipe into this shape to allow the string to slide over the nock.

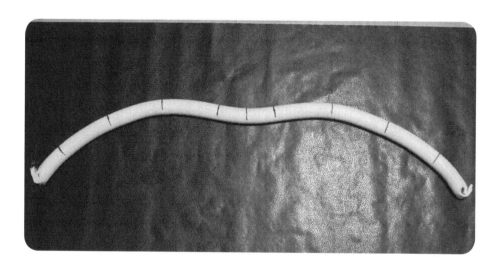

Repeat on the other limb.

The Bison

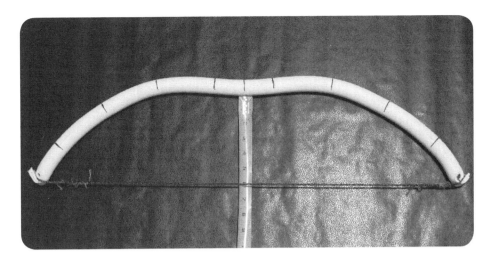

This bow can be braced to a full six inches because of the way the string is attached.

Here it is at full draw, which is twenty four inches.

FULL DRAW BOWS

Many types of plastic, PVC included, are very flexible. They can bend with little ill effect, sometimes bending a great many times before even beginning to fatigue. One of the downsides to this flexibility is that a piece of PVC will bend more readily than a piece of wood of the same dimensions (even if hollow).

This can mean two things. First off, this means that a wooden bow six feet long and pulling sixty pounds will pull considerably less if made from a solid piece of PVC (and be much heavier) because the plastic is so flexible. Wood is much less flexible than plastic, and wood can only bend so far before failure. PVC can be bent much, much further before failing. So this means that, secondly, to match the weight of pull of the wood bow, the PVC bow must either have a lot more material (imagine a bow weighing ten pounds) or be much shorter.

For these bows, which are made from only one piece of PVC piping that is not tillered in any way, the length reduction is not as harsh. The reason is that these bows only bend near the center, whereas the traditional wooden longbow would be bending evenly along its limbs. These characteristics make PVC pipe good for bows that are between three and a half to five feet long, making them perfect for replicating some of the more exotic Asiatic composite bows.

A good example, the Forest Cobra, is a short, recurved bow based off of the composite bows used in parts of China, and at full draw resembles the short Turkish flight bows. Traditionally made of sinew and horn over a wooden core, these composite bows were short and were perfect for use on horseback or on foot for hunting and war. This bow falls around the thirty-five to fifty-five draw weight range, and is second only to the King Cobra in comfort. Though at almost a foot shorter, this is a great bow that can be taken just about anywhere.

The Desert Serpent is a short bow of a simplified design similar to those used by the nomadic Scythians, as well as some bows from Egypt. It is a fast-stacking bow of around fifty pounds of pull, and while it shoots relatively well, the bow is quite noisy. The string resting over the nocks causes a hollow thump every time the bow is fired. These make very good fishing bows (there can be fish in a desert, you never know).

The easiest bow to shoot is the King Cobra, a four and a half foot long bow of forty to fifty pounds of pull. It is based off the larger bows of the 13th century Mongols, which probably did not have string bridges. It is a smooth shooting bow with little hand shock, and while it still is noisy, is quieter than the others. Because of its length, it can be pulled to longer draws up to thirty-six inches, bringing its weight closer to sixty pounds. It is a little on the heavy side, but still makes a good practice or loaner bow.

The final bow is the Divine Wind, a bow based off of the Japanese yumi hankyu, or half bow. Unlike the seven foot yumi daikyu, this bow is roughly five feet long, though still can be pulled to thirty-six inches or more. It is a heavier weight bow, and the off-center handle actually makes it a very smooth shooter , though it is a bit long. The Japanese longbow was traditionally used on horseback, as the short lower limb allowed the incredibly long bow to be maneuvered fairly easily.

While they work fairly well, their accuracy and speed will be self evident once they are shot. They are very slow and rather unpredictable as far as target groupings go. These are good bows for LARP and medieval re-enactment combat, just be sure to match the poundage to your group's limits. Just make sure to keep them out of the sun, or at least cover them up (duct tape or leather are good options, depending on how period you want to be).

THE IMPOSSIBLE BOW

Forest Cobra

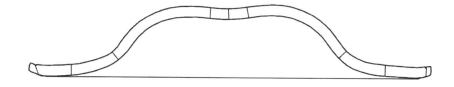

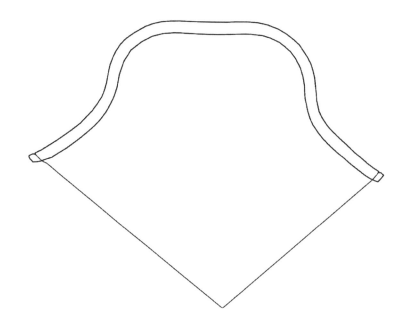

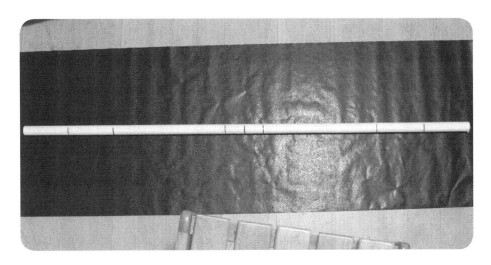

Start with a four foot length of 3/4" pipe. Mark the center and two inches from center in both directions. Mark five and ten inches in from both ends.

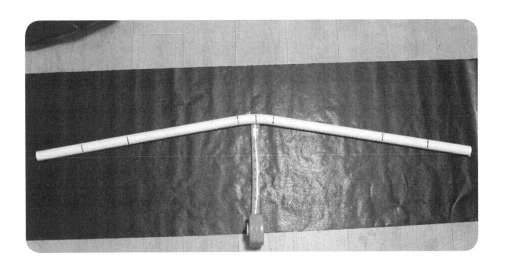

Heat the very center, and bend the pipe back until the tips reach three inches.

The Impossible Bow

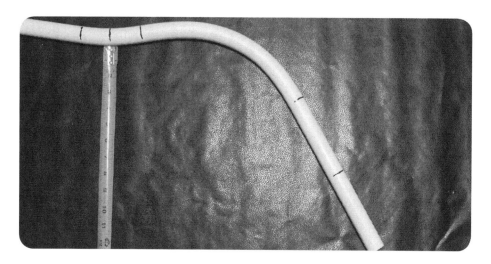

Flip the pipe over, then heat the whole section between the handle and the mark ten inches in from the end. Bend this back until the ten inch mark hits about three inches.

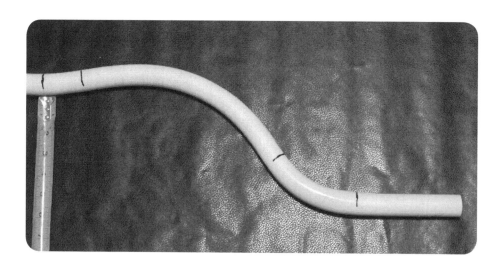

Heat the section between the five and ten inch marks, bending it forward until the five inch end section is straight.

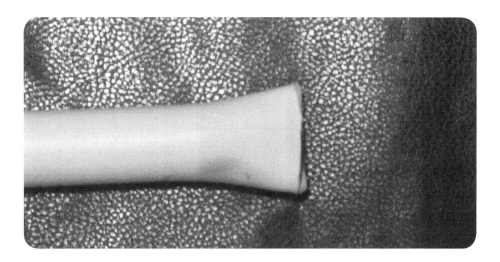

Heat the very end of the tip and flatten it.

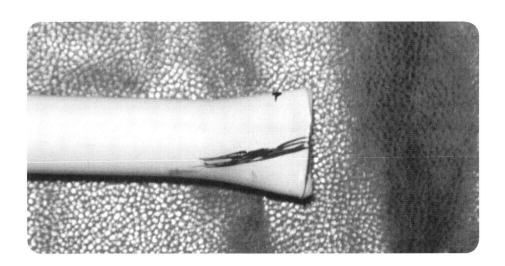

Mark half an inch in from the end, on the back of the bow and mark draw a line that follows the curve of the top of the flattened end, like in the picture.

The Impossible Bow

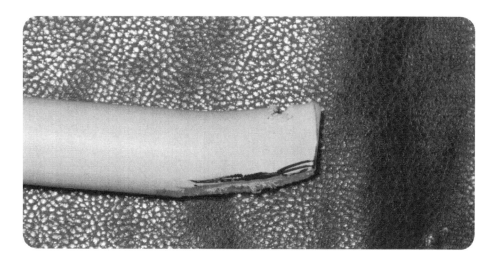

Cut your nock at the half an inch mark and cut the line you drew on the belly side of the nock.

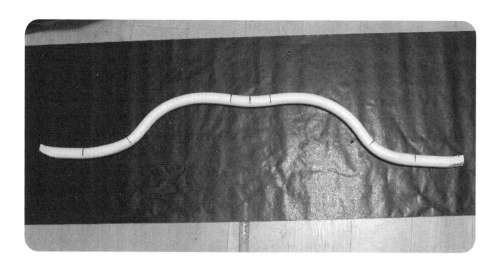

Repeat steps three to seven on the other limb, so that the bow looks like this.

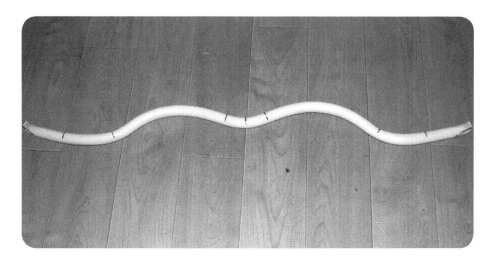

Heat the handle, then bend towards the back of the bow until the handle lines up with the tips. Make sure the bow is on a flat surface.

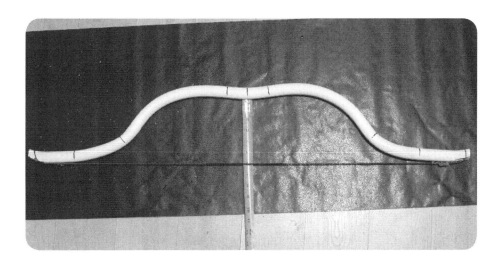

String the bow up to a brace of six inches. The brace height can be as high as eight inches. On this bow, a higher brace will result in more stack in the draw, resulting in a higher draw weight.

THE IMPOSSIBLE BOW

Here it is at full draw. This is one of the most comfortable of the bent PVC bows to shoot, next to the king cobra.

Desert Serpent

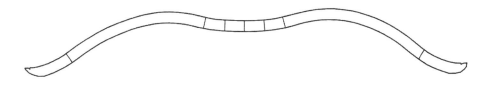

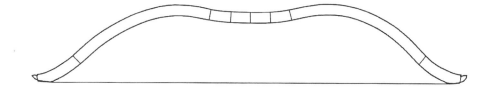

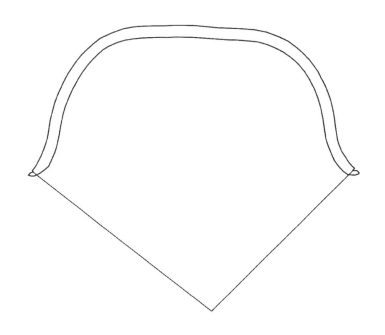

THE IMPOSSIBLE BOW

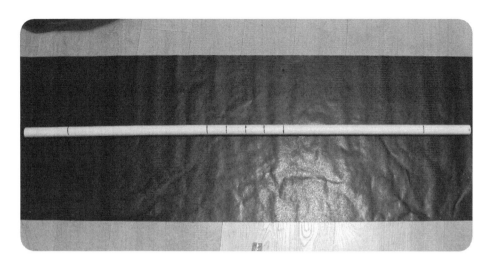

Start with a four foot length of 3/4" PVC pipe. Mark the center, two inches from center, and four inches from center in both directions. Mark five inches in from both ends.

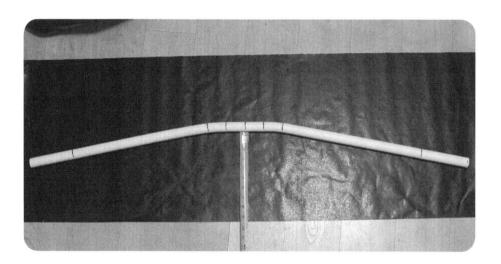

Heat the area between the two and four inch marks on both sides of the handle and flex these back until the tips hit about three inches.

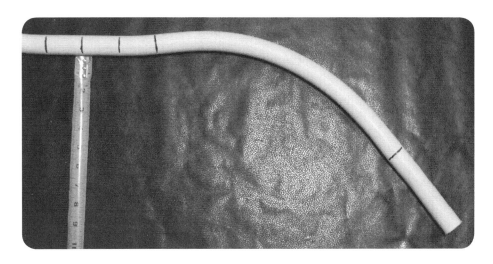

Flip the pipe over, then heat the area between the four inch handle mark and the five inch end mark. Bend this area down till the five inch mark reaches about five inches.

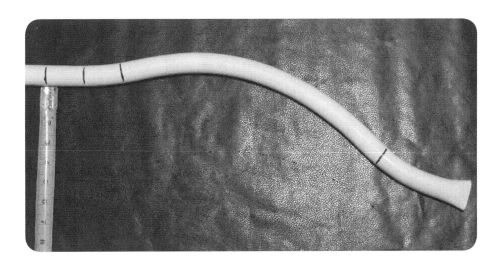

Heat and flatten the very end of the pipe. Then heat the entire end section and curve it upwards until the uppermost point of the end reaches five to six inches.

THE IMPOSSIBLE BOW

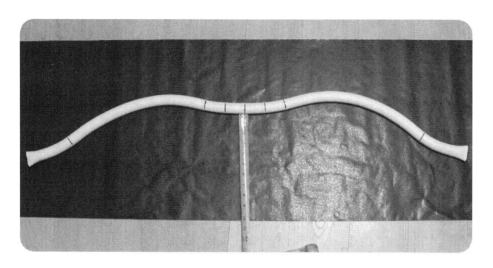

Repeat on the other limb.

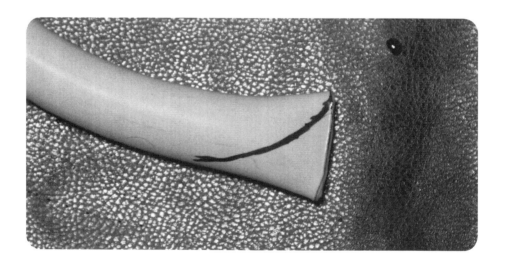

We'll be cutting away some of the tip for the string to sit, so draw a line that cuts away the bottom part of the flattened tip.

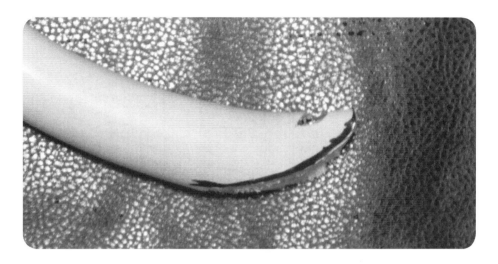

Cut along the line and also cut a notch for the string to sit in half an inch in from the end.

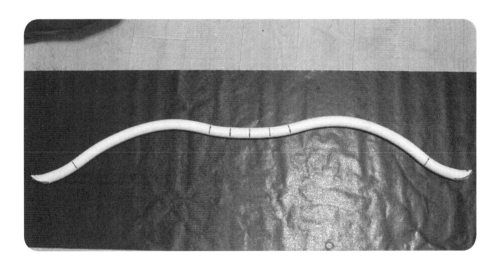

Repeat on the other end.

THE IMPOSSIBLE BOW

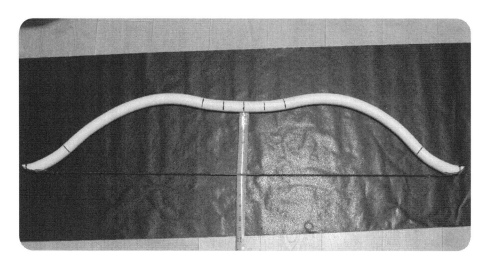

String the bow up to a six inch brace. This bow will handle up to an eight inch brace.

Here's the bow at full draw.

NICHOLAS TOMIHAMA

King Cobra

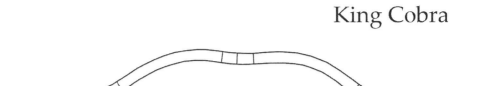

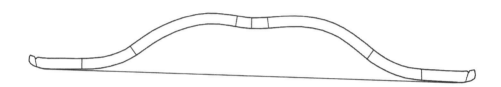

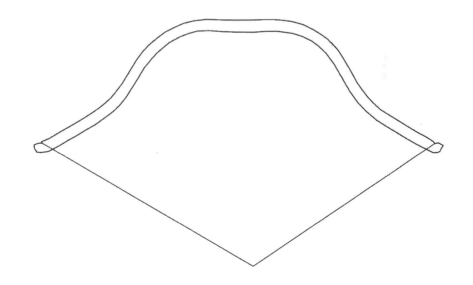

The Impossible Bow

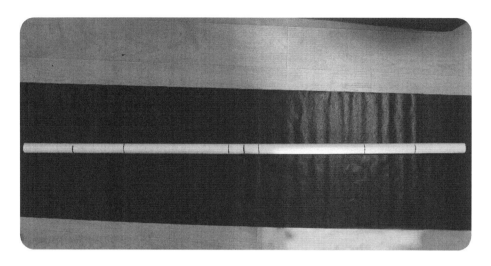

Start with a five foot length of 1" pipe. Mark the center and two inches from center. Then mark six and twelve inches in from either end.

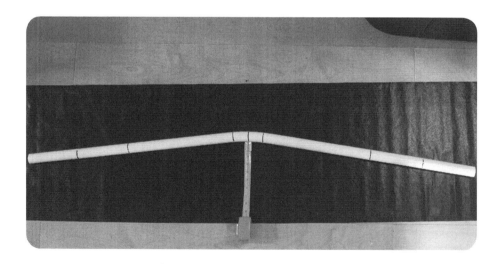

Heat and bend the handle down until the tips reach three inches.

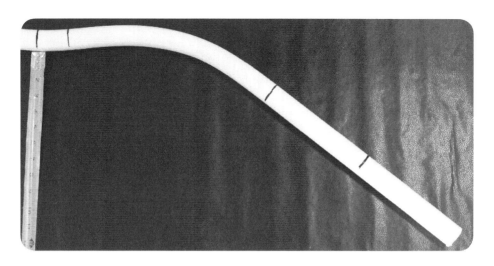

Flip the pipe over and then heat the section between the handle and the twelve inch end mark. Bend this down until the twelve inch mark reaches about three inches.

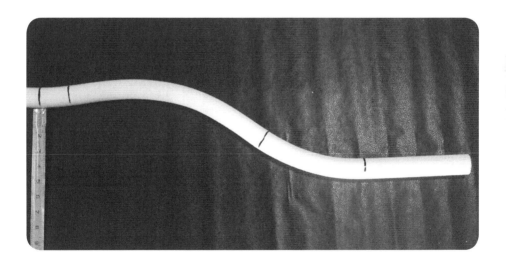

Heat and bend the section between the twelve and six inch marks up until the end section sits horizontal to the rest of the bow.

THE IMPOSSIBLE BOW

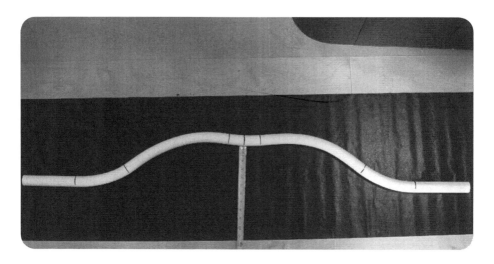

Repeat on the other limb.

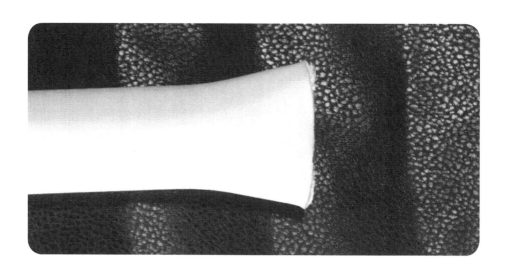

Next, flatten the end.

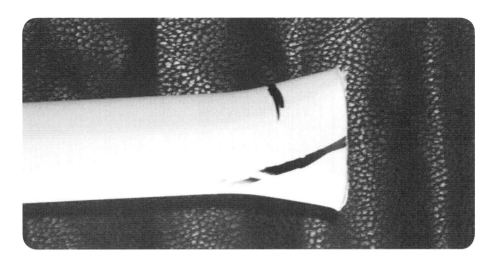

Mark an inch in from the end on the back of the bow and then mark a line cutting away the bottom curve of the flattened tip.

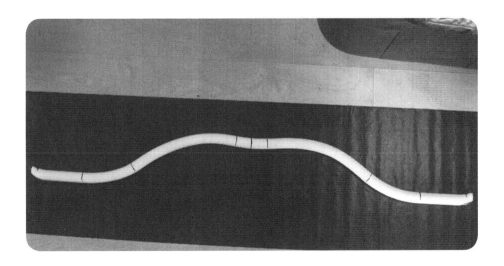

Cut the nock and tip for both ends.

THE IMPOSSIBLE BOW

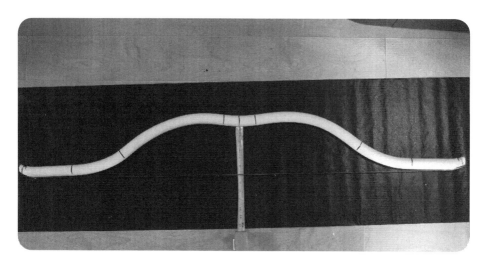

String the bow up to a six inch brace. This bow can take up to a ten inch brace, but six to eight inches work the best.

Here's the bow at full draw. It is a smooth drawing bow, roughly forty five pounds.

King Cobra

Nicholas Tomihama

Divine Wind

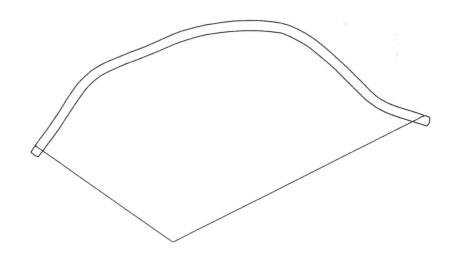

THE IMPOSSIBLE BOW

Start with a six foot length of pipe. Place two marks, separating the pipe into three equal sections, each two feet long. Take both end sections and mark them into three smaller sections. Mark four inches up from one of the two foot sections, which will become a handle.

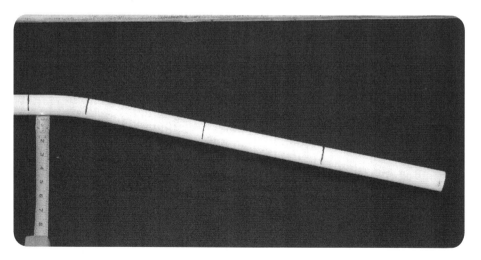

Heat the handle section and bend it down until the very end reaches five inches.

Divine Wind

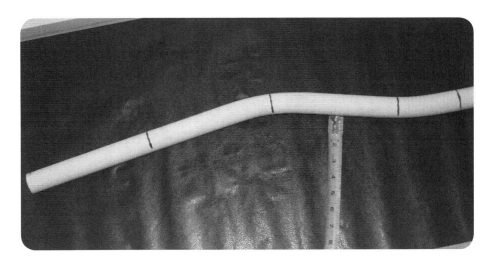

Flip the bow over. Rotate the bow so that the section that was bent forward is now horizontal. Heat the second line in from the end and bend it down until it reaches five and a half inches.

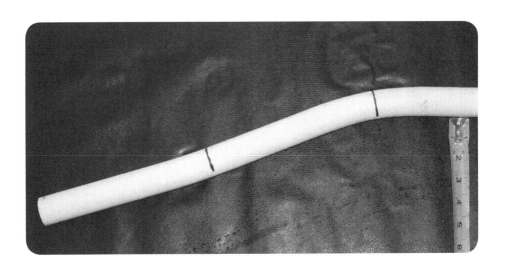

Heat the first mark in from the end and bend it up until the very tip reaches five inches.

The Impossible Bow

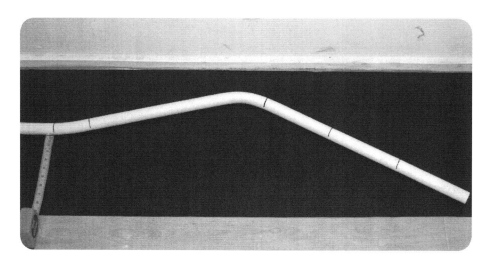

Keeping the bow in the same place, heat the third line from the end and bend it down until the tip reaches eight inches.

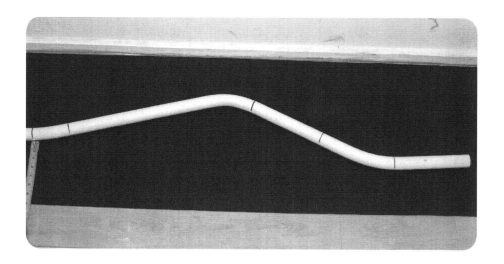

Heat and bend the second section from the end and bend it up, till the second section rests at four inches.

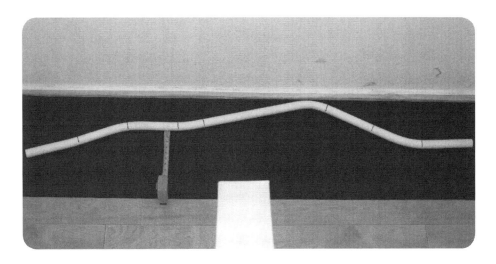

Here's the bow after all the bends are made.

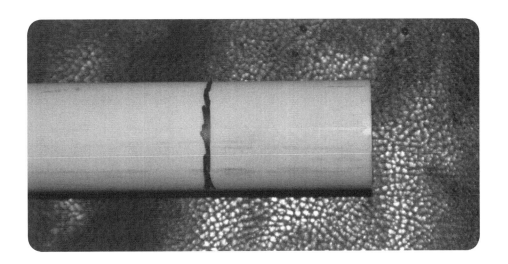

Measure and mark two inches in from the end.

THE IMPOSSIBLE BOW

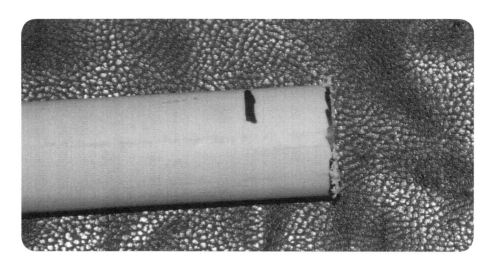

Cut the end off, then mark an inch in from the end.

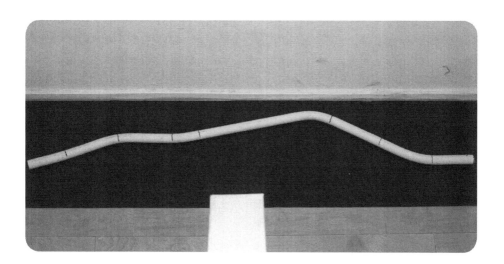

Repeat on both ends, then cut the notch for the nocks at the one inch mark from each end.

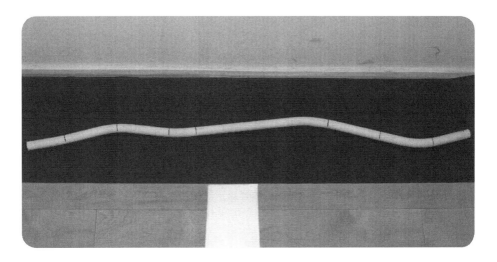

Heat the main bend on the third mark from the end on the right limb and bend it forward until the tips and the handle for a straight line.

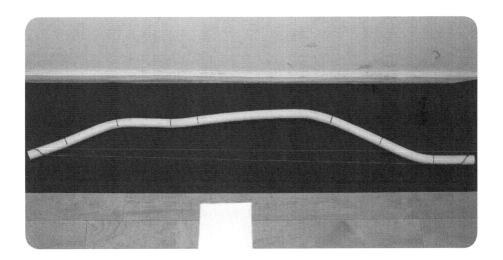

String the bow up so that the brace height is six inches measured from the forward part of the handle.

The Impossible Bow

Here is the bow at full draw. It is not as long as most traditional Japanese bows, but is still very tall. Be aware of its length when shooting indoors or walking with it while holding the handle.

Nicholas Tomihama
Reinforcing Handles

Because of the nature of these simple bows, their handles are under a lot of stress. All of the flex in the PVC pipe happens very close to the handle, so even a small crack or cut in that area could be catastrophic. PVC is a soft material, and the repeated abrasion of an arrow being fired can eventually wear a groove in the handle. If left unchecked, this could eventually fail, causing the bow to collapse at best and shatter into razor shards at the worst.

To prevent a handle failure, it is a good idea to at least cover the area where the arrow passes. The easiest way to do this is to glue or tape on a piece of leather or tough plastic where the arrow passes, or to glue on a commercial arrow rest. In this section we'll go over one way to protect the handle.

This a good handle for these bows, as it not only protects the bow, but it also protects your hand. By wrapping the PVC with fiberglass strapping tape, the likelihood of the bow snapping decreases. The strapping tape also keep the shards from cutting you if the bow ever does explode. The foam padding also cuts down on the shock and vibration these bows have when shot.

This type of handle reinforcement can be done quickly and with little expense, which fits into the whole theme of this book. It does have a very home-made look about it, so other methods can give the same protection with more pleasing results. Leather or tough cordage wrapped around the handle is usually enough to protect your bow and yourself.

THE IMPOSSIBLE BOW

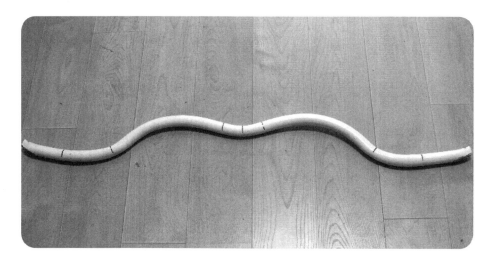

Start out with the bow you wish to put a handle on. If you haven't shot the bow yet, now's the time to decide which limb you want to be the top.

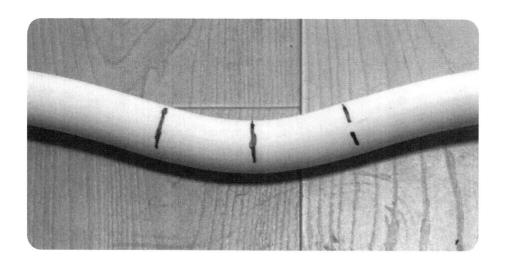

When strung, the bottom limb should be the one that has slightly less bend in it, as it will have to bend more than the top limb when the bow is fully drawn.

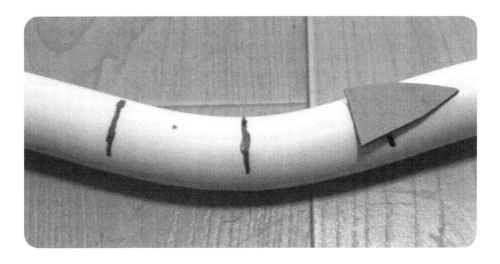

Place a triangle of leather or heavy plastic over the place where the arrow will pass over.

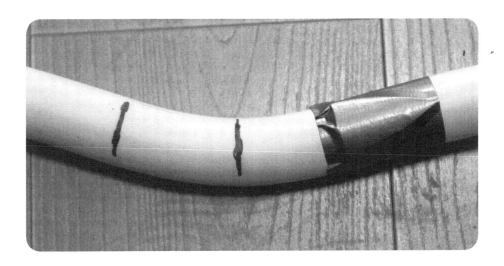

Wrap the triangle of leather or plastic with a strip of duct tape or similar tape to reinforce the area.

THE IMPOSSIBLE BOW

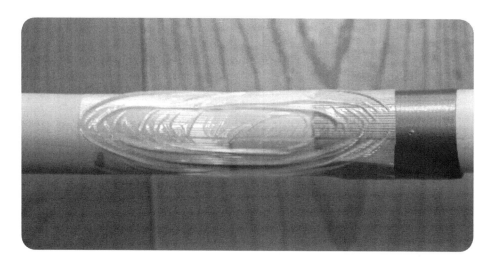

From the top, or the back of the bow, place a strip of fiberglass strapping tape that covers where your hand sits on the handle.

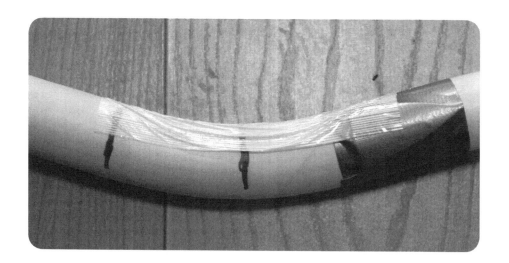

Here is its from the side.

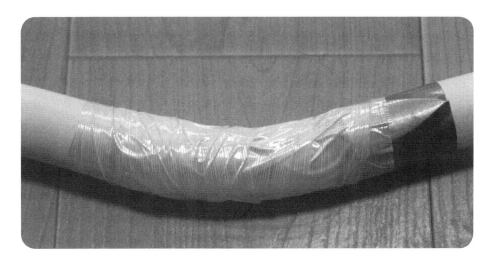

Wrap strapping tape around the handle at least once. Since we will be padding it, too much tape will make the handle very large.

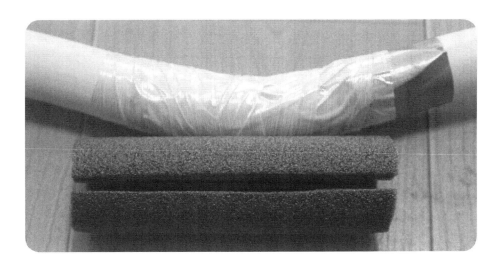

Cut a piece of foam the length of your handle. A good source of foam is closed cell pipe insulation, which can be found in the plumbing section of most hardware stores.

THE IMPOSSIBLE BOW

Place the foam over the handle of the bow, placing the open side on the front of the handle, AKA the back of the bow.

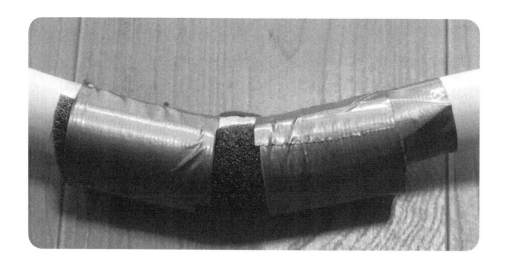

Wrap the foam in a little bit of duct tape to keep it in place.

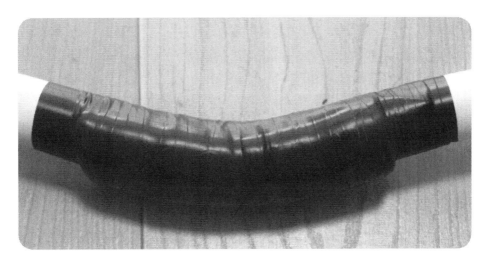

Finish the handle with the tape of your choice. Good quality electrical tape will give the handle a nice, slightly tacky grip without stretching too much or getting too sticky. Be sure to evenly overlap the foam as it may squish out of any uneven, open spots.

CHAPTER THREE -
BANDED KRAIT

When designing a bow out of PVC, tiller becomes a problem. Unless you want to cut the pipe apart and re-laminate it similar to an Asiatic composite bow, there aren't many options. There is one good method, however, that produces good results, although results in an odd shape for a bow.

Because PVC pipe is just that, a hollow pipe, it does not bend the same as if it were a flat sheet. The round cross section lends stiffness to the pipe. If you actually flatten the pipe, it suddenly loses much of its stiffness. By exploiting this property, it is possible to tiller an all PVC bow by simply flattening it more at the tips than at the handle, and keeping the handle full-thickness to make it stiff and unbending.

By keeping the handle stiff, this improves the shot, and allows the handle to be pushed slightly off-center to allow for less distortion in the shot. The bow's limbs also bend more evenly, allowing it to work more like a "traditional" bow. When the limbs are flattened, the overall pull of the bow goes down as the load is distributed more evenly across the limbs, so any diameter smaller than 1 inch pipe will produce a bow that is very weak.

This particular bow is short, only around forty-four inches when strung, and has a peak draw weight of around seventy pounds. The draw is smooth, with no stack until beyond thirty inches. At this size and draw weight, this bow would make a good bow for hunting, as it does not have the hollow sound of other PVC bows, and also because it draws evenly, gaining a consistent amount of weight per inch of draw, like a good longbow.

While this bow does not look much like a traditional bow from the back or belly, it resembles some bows of the native tribes of the Western North America. This bow does not work in the same way as these bows, as it does not bend at the handle. It also has static tips that do not unfurl when the bow is drawn.

The instructions for this bow push it to its shortest safe length, therefore its maximum draw weight without quick failure. If you prefer a lower draw weight, simply start out with a longer piece of pipe. The draw weight should drop about four pounds for every inch the bow is lengthened, making this a versatile bow that can reach lower weights of fifty to forty five pounds at less than five feet long. If done in 3/4" pipe and starting at forty-eight inches, this design makes a fun little thirty pound bow.

To fit the bow material, the finished bow is covered in duct tape and PVC tape (electrical insulating tape). If you prefer, the bow can be finished any number of ways including painting, wrapping with cord, or even covering with leather, which allows the bow to look as if it isn't made of PVC pipe. The bow can also be left bare, though the PVC will be susceptible to UV light. While the handle can be covered, it is not absolutely necessary on this particular bow.

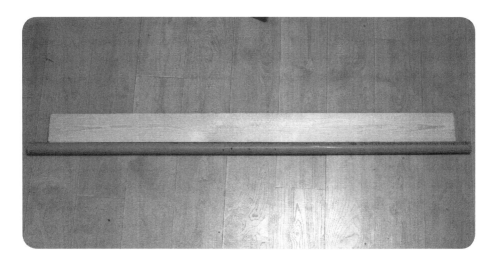

Start with a 1 inch PVC pipe, fifty-two inches long. The pipe can be any type, though UV-resistant PVC conduit works best. Also get a four foot long board for flattening the limbs.

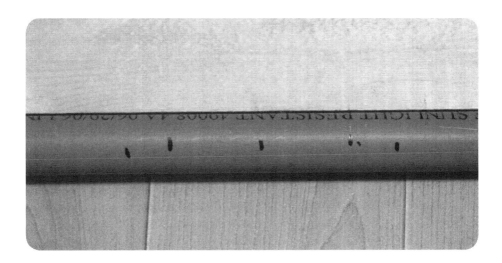

Mark the center of the pipe. This is the little double mark in the picture. Mark two inches down, which will be the center of the handle, and two inches down from that, ending the handle. Mark an inch on either side of the handle.

THE IMPOSSIBLE BOW

Prepare the flattening board by placing two small pieces of wood 3/4 of an inch thick. This will give the required taper from the handle to the tips of the bow. Make sure the flattening board is on a smooth, flat surface as any waves or bumps will be transferred to the bow.

Begin heating one limb over the heat source, turning it and moving it so that it does not burn to turn yellow.

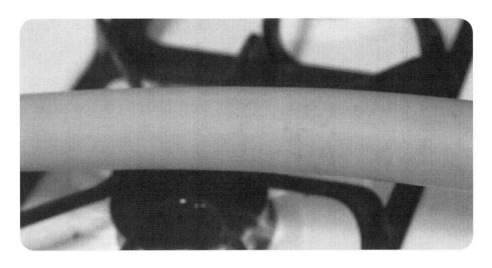

Keep heating until the whole limb is soft and can easily be bent and flattened.

Quickly place the limb under the flattening board and apply pressure. A good way to do this is to stand on the board, as it takes a good amount of pressure to flatten 1 inch pipe.

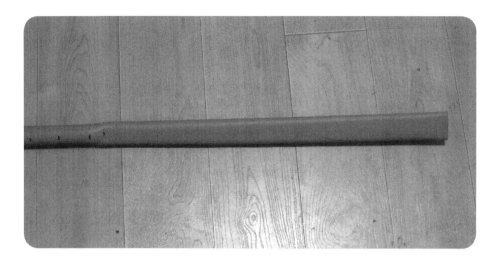

Here is what the flattened limb should look like. Width-wise, this is unusual for most bows, as the limbs are usually not widest at the very tips.

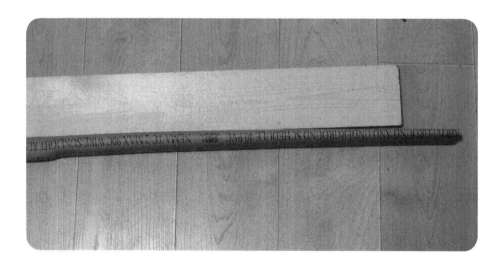

This is how the limb should look like from the side, starting off thick near the handle and flattening out near the tip.

Flatten the other limb.

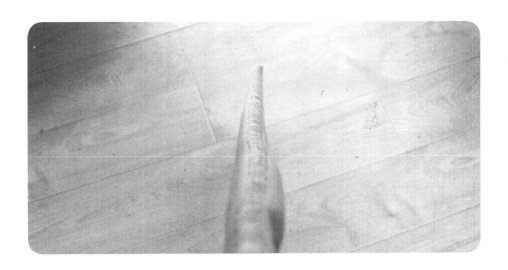

A view of the taper looking down from the handle, on the side of the bow.

THE IMPOSSIBLE BOW

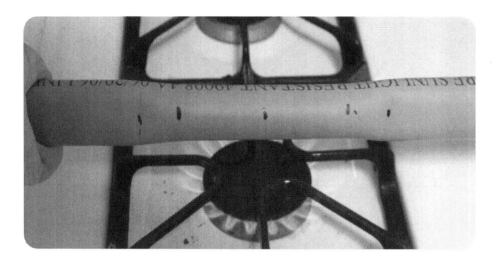

Heat the handle until it is easily bent and can be pressed.

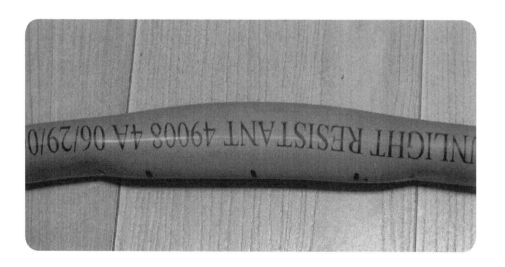

Press the handle section, making it swell near the handle's center. Bend it slightly back towards the belly so that the belly side of the handle is flat, the back side curved.

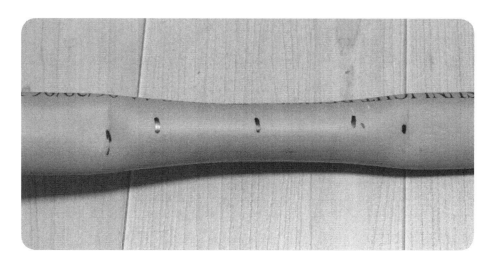

Here's the handle from the belly side.

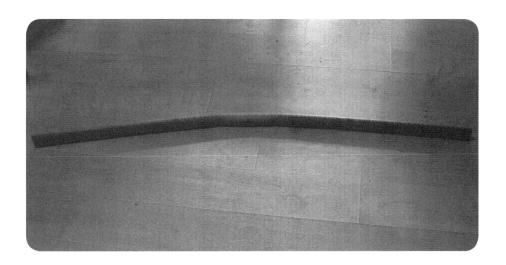

This is what the bow should look like at this stage.

The Impossible Bow

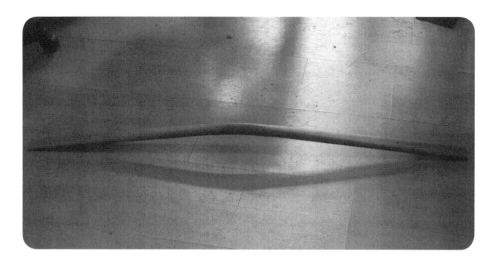

At this point, the tips of the bow should be set back about two to three inches away from the handle.

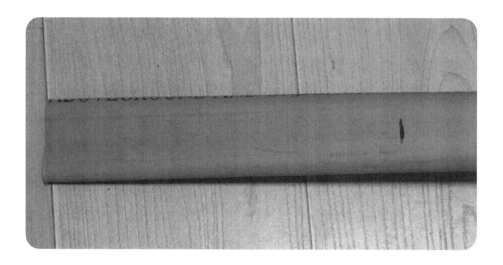

Mark eight inches from one end.

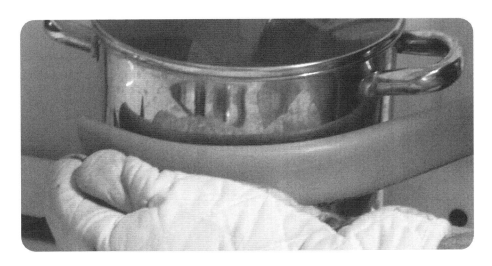

Heat the end up until it flexes, but not so much that the pipe puff up to its regular size. Take an eight inch diameter pot or bucket and flex the eight inch area around it, holding until the pipe takes the shape.

This is what the tip looks like after reflexing. This harsh recurve is to make use of the fact that the tip will not bend on a bow like this.

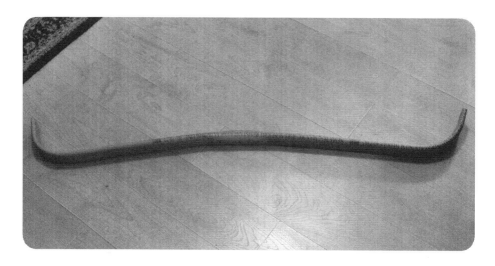

Repeat the reflexing on the other limb. Because one limb is a little longer than the other, the bow may look a little lopsided for now.

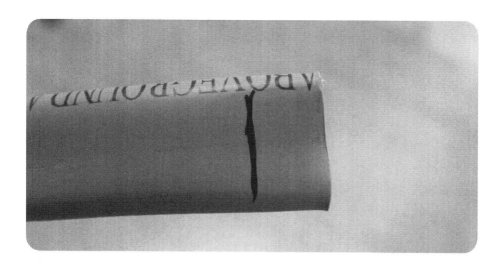

Mark half an inch in from the end of the bow.

Cut half an inch in from either side, then follow the half an inch line in from each side to create a pin nock.

Go back to the handle and heat up the areas near the handle, which were once squashed. After they get soft, they will puff back up, this will keep the bow from collapsing at this spot.

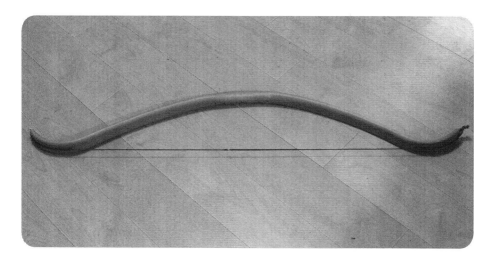

Now string the bow up. As long as both limbs were flattened evenly, the bow should have an even bend to it. In this case, the right limb is a little weaker than the other, because it is shorter.

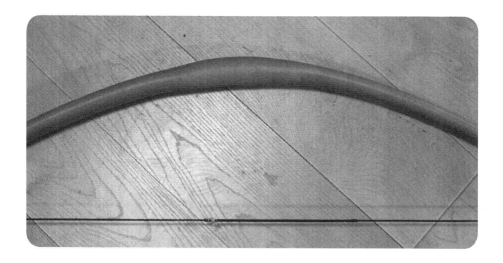

You can see it is also a little thinner near the handle. This type of weakness can appear anywhere, and must be fixed now or the bow (this one is under a lot of stress) could collapse.

To strengthen that spot, heat it up gently until the spot starts to puff up a little. The puffed up area will now be stronger than before. Be careful not too let it puff up too much, as new flaws may arise.

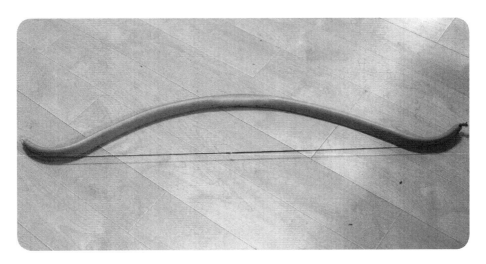

Once the bow is evened out, it should look like this when strung to a brace of around six inches.

THE IMPOSSIBLE BOW

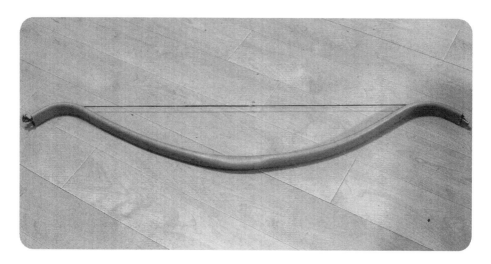

Here's the bow from the back side. The bow is now finished and ready to shoot. Read on if you want to finish the bow off with a decorative duct tape covering. You can really do whatever you want from here on. Let your imagination run wild.

To finish the bow with duct tape and electrical tape with a striped finish, start by laying one strip of black duct tape on the belly of the bow. This strip should go from the handle to near the tip, off center so that there is complete coverage on the belly of the bow.

Smooth down the edges of the cut tape, working from the inside to the outside so that there are no creases or air bubbles.

Repeat for the other edge of the limb, and then repeat on the other limb until the entire belly and handle are both covered in tape.

The Impossible Bow

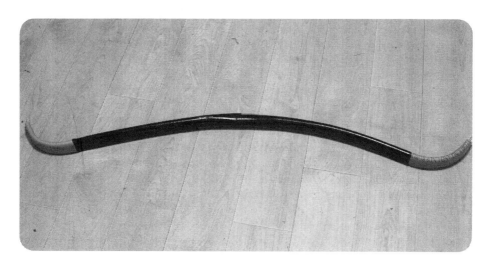

Trim the tape at the eight inch marking at each end, careful not to actually cut into the PVC.

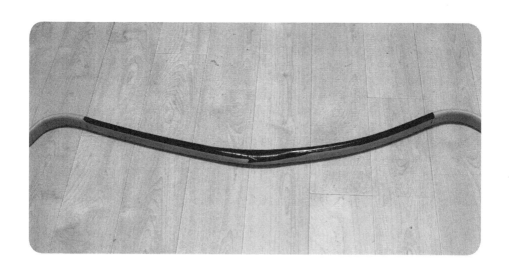

From the back, you can see how the tape overlaps, and comes up the sides of the bow.

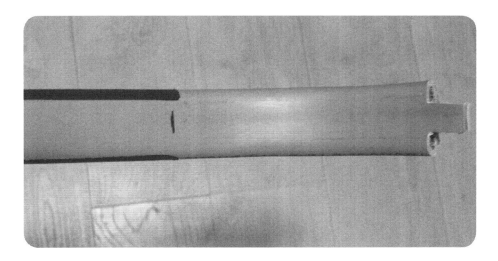

Up close, you can see where the duct tape ends. The reason for this is that the curve makes taping straight down the back and belly a little sloppy on the edges.

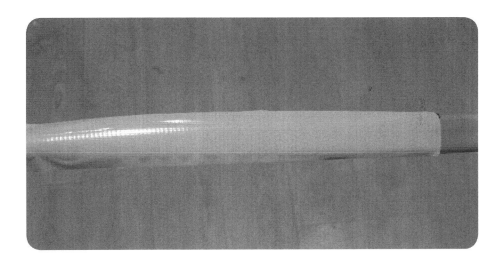

Start laying down a strip of your secondary color of duct tape across the back of the bow, centered on the bow. This one will stretch from end to end.

THE IMPOSSIBLE BOW

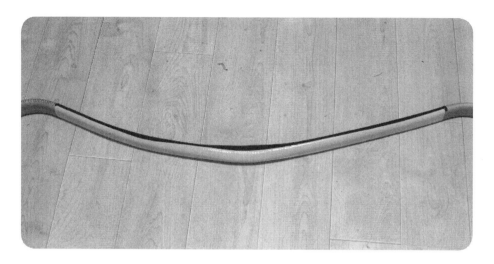

Once the tape is on, smooth it down, making sure it is centered,

Take a strip of duct tape and split it into four strips. Take one strip and start wrapping it around the end, starting where the other duct tape ends.

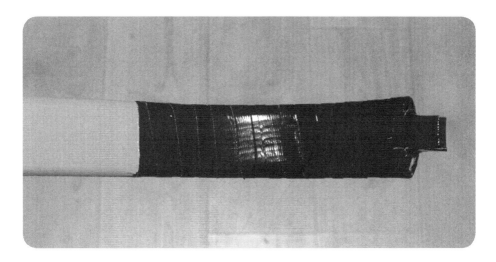

Keep winding it around the end, simply overlapping wherever one strip ends and another begins. Once at the tip, wrap the nock area from the sides, then place one piece of a strip over the end to finish it off.

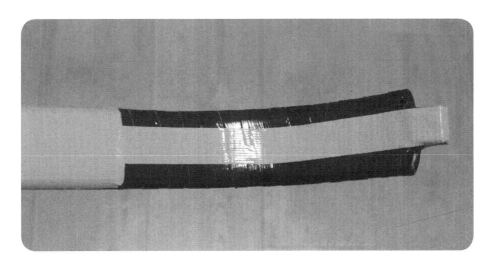

Take a strip of your secondary color duct tape 1/2 an inch wide, and run it from the back to the belly. Start it on the back, right where the secondary color ends.

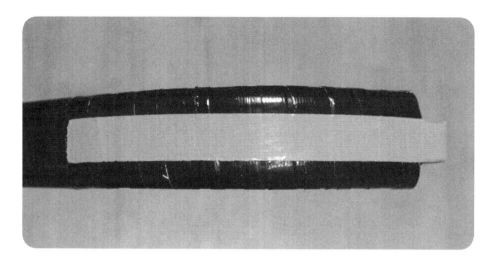

Bring the strip around the belly, ending it right where the main limb duct tape ends.

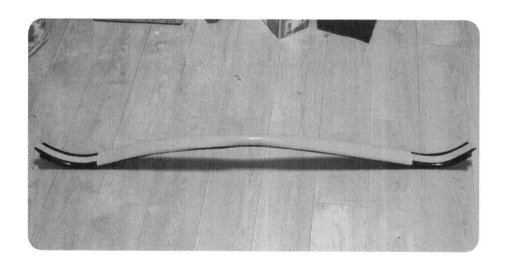

Repeat this on the other limb tip.

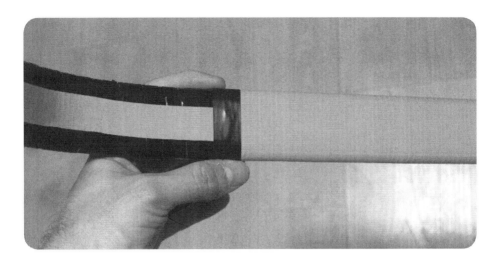

Start the electrical tape wrap at one of the tips on the back, covering the transition of the separate duct tape wraps.

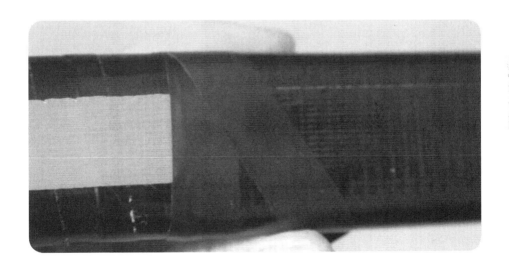

Bring the tape around and angle it roughly forty-five degrees across the belly.

THE IMPOSSIBLE BOW

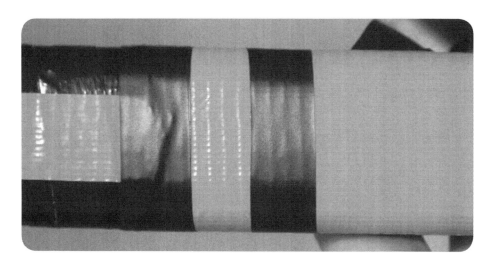

Bring the tape around, straight across the back of the bow.

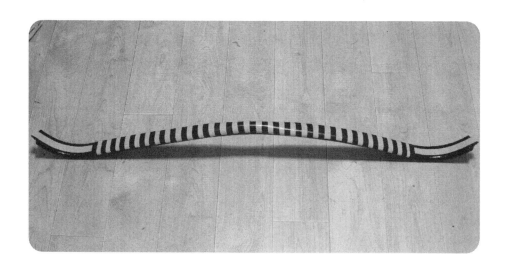

Repeat the wrap down to the other end of the bow.

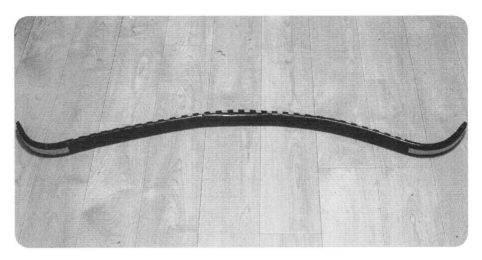

Here's the finished tape wrap from the belly side. One interesting thing about electrical tape is that if the bow is exposed to too much UV light, the PVC electrical tape will start to turn brittle, which can be an indicator of sorts to whether or not the bow should be replaced.

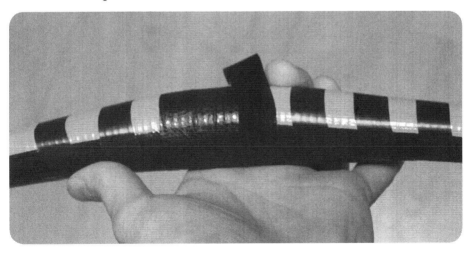

The handle can be wrapped with electrical tape, vinyl (imitation leather), or whatever else you want. Even baseball bat handle wrap and tennis racquet handle wrap works. Start your handle wrap an inch above the middle of the handle on the side of the top limb (longer limb).

The Impossible Bow

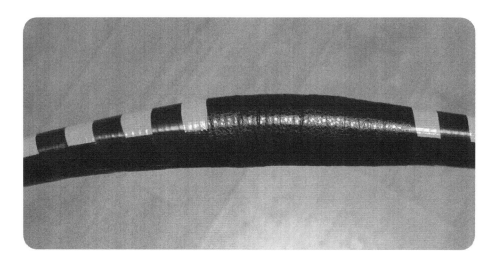

Continue the wrap down to the end of the handle area. Four to five inches is usually good enough for most hands, but whatever fits you is best.

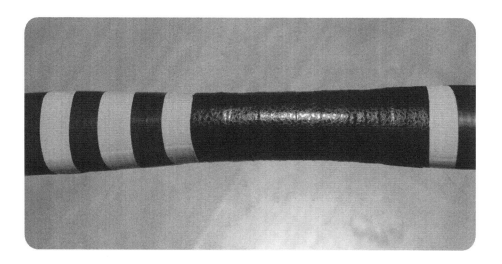

Here's the handle from the back. The arrow will rest just above the wrap, so if you want to shoot your arrows on the wrap, move the wrap up to cover that area.

Here's the finished bow at brace. This particular bow design works well with higher braces as well, an eight inch brace will help cut down on noise caused by the string hitting the recurved tips after the arrow is released.

Here is the bow at full brace. You can see that the tips stay stiff. They act like levers, making this bow comfortable with the three finger draw, even with such a short bow.

CHAPTER FOUR -
INDIGO SERPENT

As a bow material, PVC has good qualities, but so far, all the bows only vaguely resemble traditional bows in shape. Due to the nature of PVC, it works best in short bow designs, and works well in bows that don't require much in the way of tapering down the limbs. For these reasons, PVC works really well as the core for Asiatic composite bows.

This particular style of bow is based off of modern Mongolian short bows, which are in turn based off of the short Korean bow. While it is a lower weight bow, it is smooth-drawing and fast, making it a great bow for kids, target shooting, and even LARP and re-enactment. It can also be drawn clear up to back of the chin, as a Korean or Mongolian bow should be.

This bow is also unique as it has laminated siyahs or bow ears. This makes the tips non-bending, causing them to act like levers. This gives the bow good speed, even though PVC is usually on the sluggish side. This bow also has string bridges, which not only give the string a place to track when strung, but also give the arrow a little extra snap at the end of the release. Without the string bridges, this bow is very quiet.

Unlike the other bows in the book, the Indigo Serpent, named for a non-poisonous snake that has an appetite for rattlesnakes, uses some materials other than PVC for its construction. The siyahs are carved from wood, glued on, and bound with cord. The string bridges are also made of wood, and lashed onto the bow with cord, though these can be put on or taken off as needed.

This particular bow, just like the Banded Krait, it finished with duct tape. While this isn't a bad option, a more authentic look can be obtained by wrapping the limbs in leather or cord. Or, if you want to go more traditional Mongolian, a layer of paper can be applied to the surface with glue, like paper mache or decopauge. This can then be either left as is or painted. Either way, this makes the bow look almost exactly like a true Mongolian bow.

From brace to full draw, this is the bow that will turn heads and get attention. It's also the bow nobody will believe is made of PVC, even after shooting it. It takes a little more work than the other PVC bows, but much less than a traditional Mongolian bow. So if you've got an afternoon or two, some patience and some files, you are good to go!

THE IMPOSSIBLE BOW

Indigo Serpent

Start with a forty inch piece of 3/4 inch PVC pipe. Gray conduit works best for this bow.

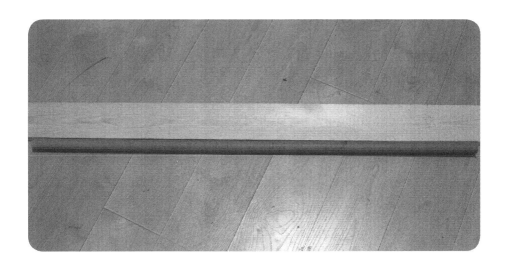

You will also need a four foot long board for flattening the limbs.

The Impossible Bow

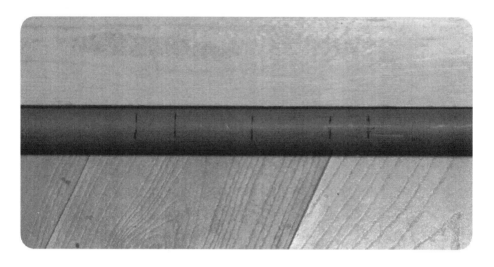

Mark the center of the pipe, two inches out from the handle on either side, and one inch out from there.

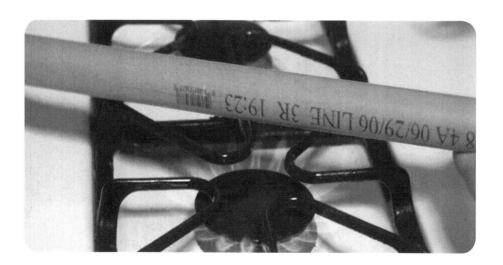

Begin heating one limb, starting at the handle. Always keep the pipe moving, making sure you don't stay in one spot for very long.

Shaping the PVC Core

A good way to do it is to slowly turn the pipe over, pulling it down about an inch every rotation.

Keep this going until you reach the end, then return to the top and start again.

The Impossible Bow

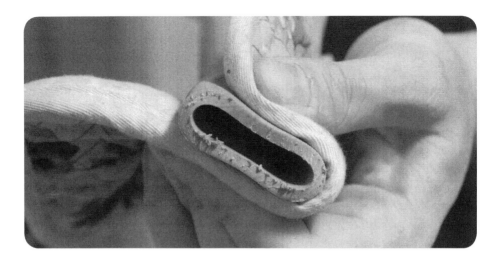

Keep heating the pipe until it become pliable and easily flattened like this.

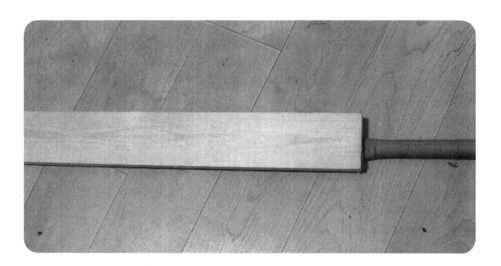

Once the limb is soft enough, place it under the board and flatten the limb. Standing on the board is usually enough to flatten the limb.

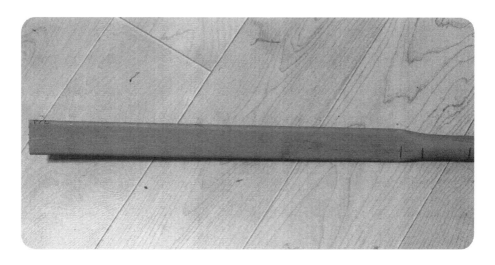

Here's what the limb should look like when flattened.

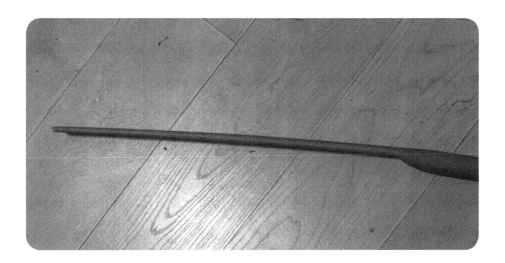

Because of how long the board is, the limb will taper slightly from the handle to the tip.

The Impossible Bow

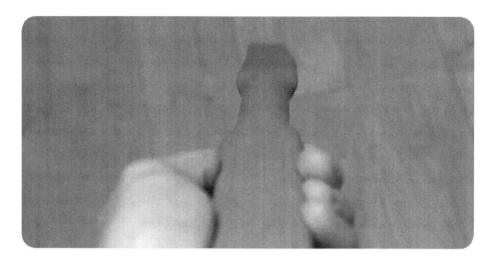

If the limb is a little crooked like this, where the tip goes way off to one side, it needs to be heated up again.

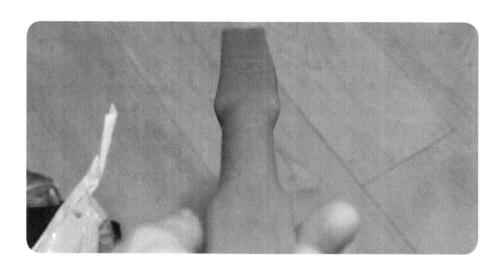

As long as the end lines up with the handle it will be fine.

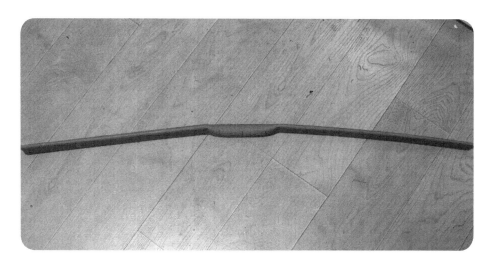

Here is what the bow should look like after both limbs are flattened.

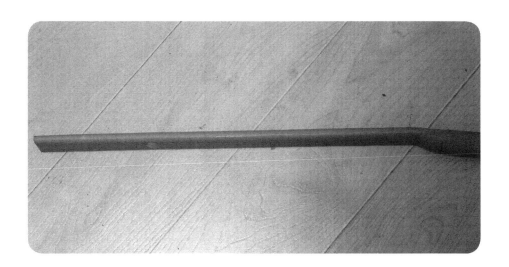

Here's a close up of one limb.

THE IMPOSSIBLE BOW

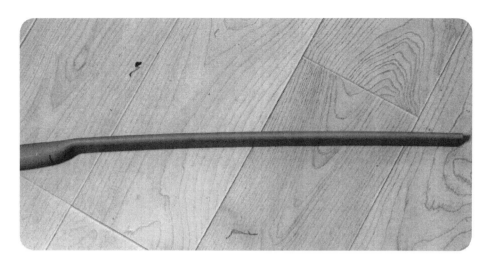

And the other. Any differences in thickness or taper can be fixed later when the bow is first strung.

Next, heat up the handle within both handle marks.

Be sure to keep the bow moving so the PVC does not burn.

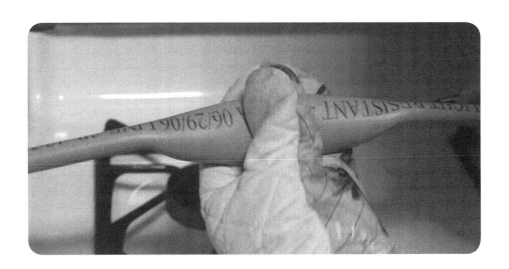

Once the handle is soft, press it together to make the handle more oval.

The Impossible Bow

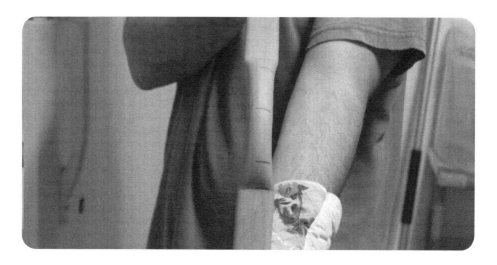

Once the bow is pressed a little, make sure to line the limbs up and bend the handle towards the back of the bow.

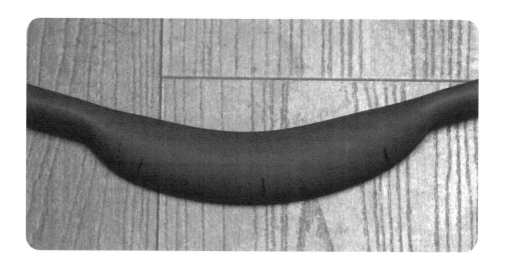

The bend in the handle should be about this much. It can be a little off, as this will be fine-tuned later.

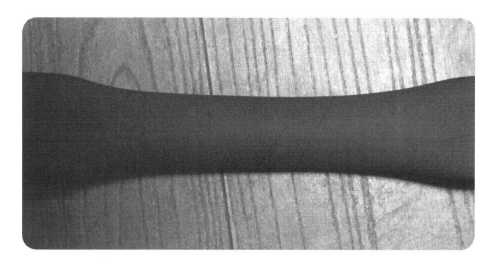

The handle from the back.

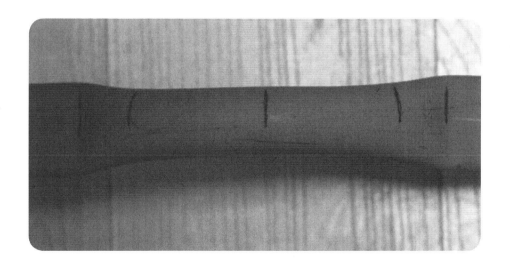

From the belly.

The Impossible Bow

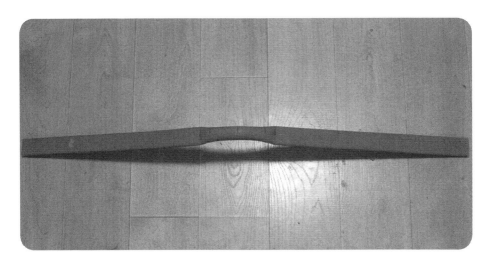

The limbs should line up on both sides.

After the handle has been reflexed, this is what the bow should look like, more or less

To start the siyahs, pick a straight-grained piece of hard wood, one foot long. Maple, oak, hickory, walnut, ash, and many other strong woods work well. Poplar, if you can find a nice, straight grained piece, will work very well as it is quite light. Mark a line on the halfway (six inch) point.

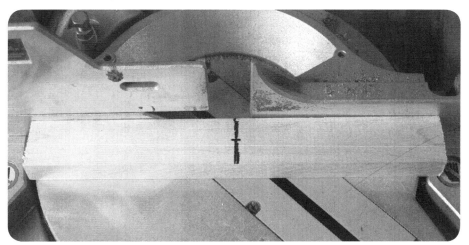

Line the wood up in a miter saw or in a miter box at forty-five degrees.

The Impossible Bow

Make sure the saw will cut the wood into two equal pieces.

Cut the pieces in half at a forty-five degree angle.

Measure 3/4 of an inch on the flat end of the piece of wood, and draw a line down to where the angled cut starts. Draw a line from the end of the line to the point of the angled cut, like in the picture. Cut this out, slightly curving along the inner angle.

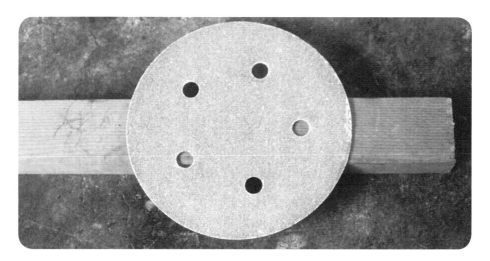

Take a piece of sandpaper and place on a flat surface.

THE IMPOSSIBLE BOW

Sand the angled end of the siyah, making sure to keep it flat. It also helps to only sand in one direction, as going back and forth may round the bottom.

Make sure both sides are flat.

Making and Gluing the Siyahs

Lightly sand the ends of the PVC pipe on the back side to prepare for gluing.

Make sure the back is as flat as possible.

Mark the center of the end of the pipe, so that you know where to line up the siyah.

Mark the center of the siyah on the bottom.

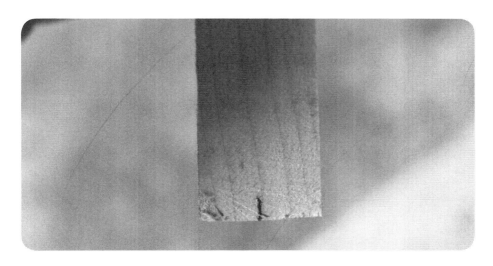

Mark it on the top as well in the center.

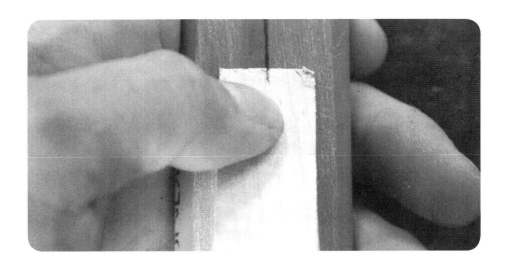

Test the joint. It should look flush from both sides.

The Impossible Bow

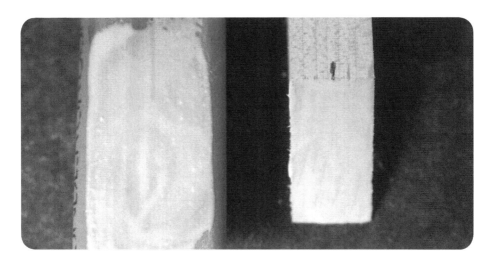

Apply epoxy or polyurethane glue to the siyah and the pipe.

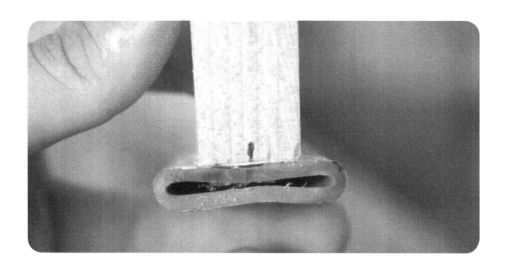

Press the two together, making sure to line up the back side

and the front side of the siyah to the pipe.

Let the glue set. It is difficult to clamp this area without the two pieces sliding, so simply hold it together until the glue gets tacky, then a couple strips of duct tape will hold it all together afterwards.

The Impossible Bow

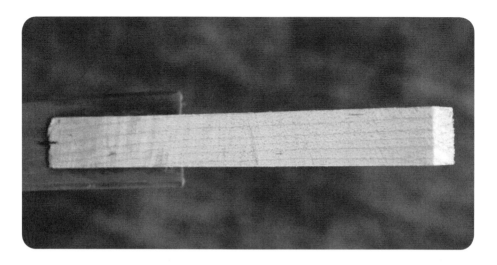

Before securing the siyah down, make sure that the tip of the siyah lines up with the bow, as the wood may be a little warped.

Repeat this on the other limb.

Making and Gluing the Siyahs

With a file or belt sander, round the siyahs down. They should look something like this from the side. They should look oval from the top.

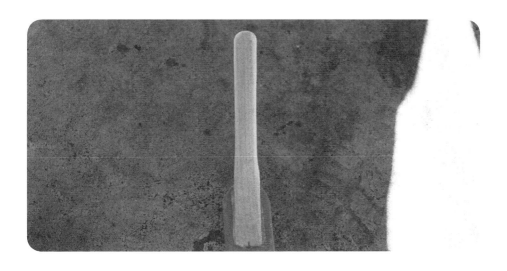

Keep the area one inch near the base of the siyah full-thickness so it will be easier to wrap.

The Impossible Bow

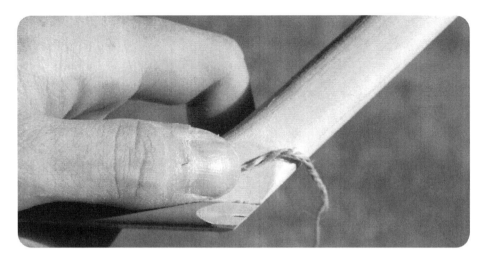

Start the wrap about where the full-thickness ends, or one inch from the bottom of the siyah. You want to use a strong cord. Hemp, linen, silk, nylon, polyester, and any other tough fiber that is not waxed will work well. You will need about ten yards per siyah.

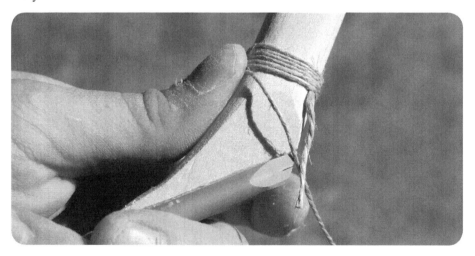

Wrap down towards the bow, going over the loose end. Once you've wrapped about this far, pull the end tight and keep wrapping.

Making and Gluing the Siyahs

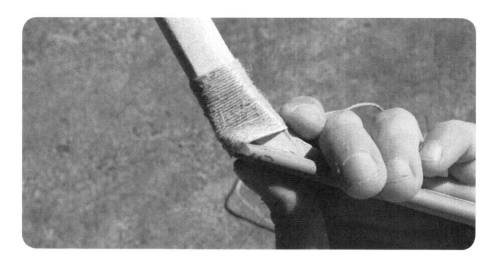

Keep on going until you reach the bottom.

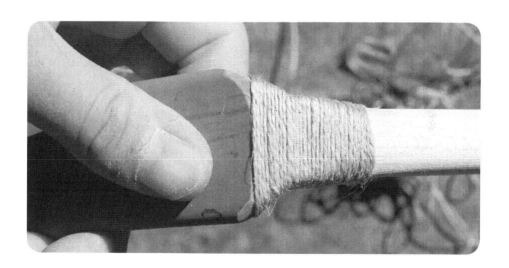

Once the wrap reaches the bottom edge, make sure everything is tight.

The Impossible Bow

Continue wrapping down the siyah, this time wrapping over the lower part of the top wrap. This allows the wrap to continue straight, gives the main wrap extra grip, and also helps keep the top wrap in place.

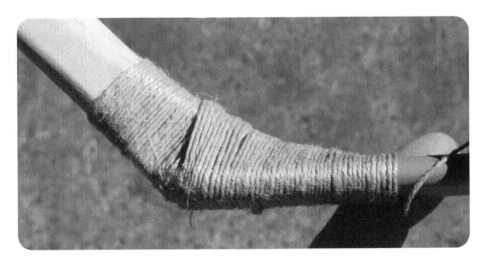

Keep wrapping until about 1/4 inch past the end of the wood siyah.

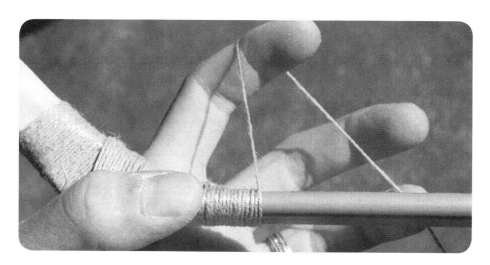

We will be doing a back-wrap now. Start by keeping about ten inches of cord attached to the wrap, and cutting it from the rest of your cord, making a loop with your finger like in the picture.

Wrap the loose end of the cord under the loop you made. You can see I am holding it down with my middle finger.

THE IMPOSSIBLE BOW

Now grab the top of the loop, and bring the loop over, like you are unwrapping the siyah. This will basically move one layer of wrap from the siyah to the end of the loop.

Do it again, making sure to not wrap over the loose end.

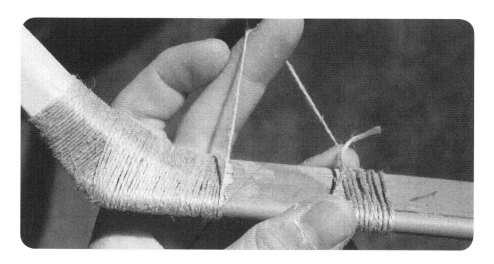

Continue wrapping until the wood from the siyah starts to show.

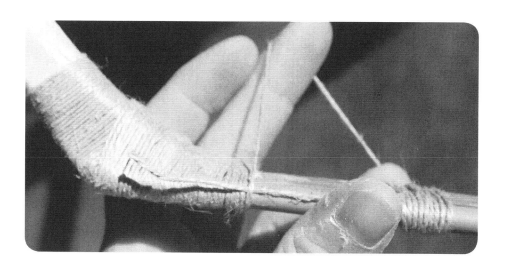

Take the loose end of the cord and tuck it under the loop like in the picture.

The Impossible Bow

Reverse the wrap until the wrap you moved is back in place. Make sure everything is tight, and make sure to not pull out the loose end, or you will have to do everything over again.

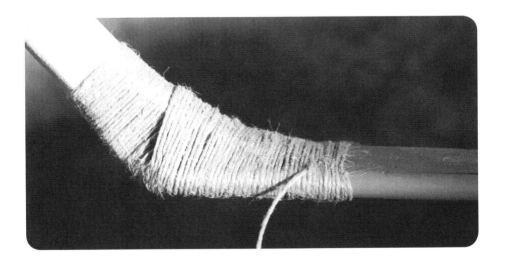

Pull the loose end through until the end of the wrap is tight. Cut the loose end flush with the rest of the wrap.

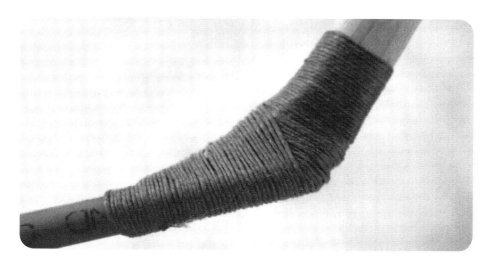

Repeat the wrap on the other siyah.

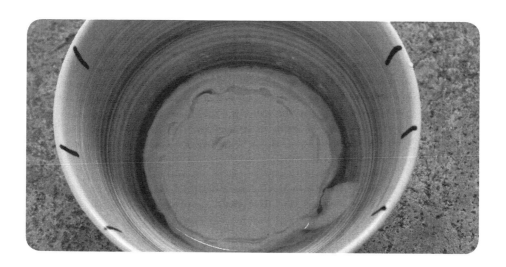

In order to waterproof the wrap and give the siyah extra strength, we will be soaking it in glue. Mix equal parts Titebond III and water in a bowl.

The Impossible Bow

Set up a place for the siyahs to dry. Here, I have two bricks on their sides to serve as a drying rack after the glue is applied. A spoon helps to apply the glue.

Pour the glue/water mixture over the top of the wrap until it does not soak in any more.

Pour glue over the side, making sure it soaks through.

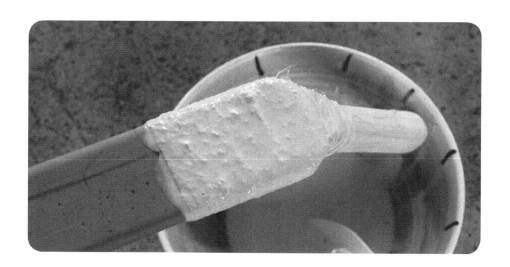

Pour glue over the belly side of the siyah.

THE IMPOSSIBLE BOW

Finish the first application by letting glue soak into the other side.

Go over the whole siyah once again to ensure it is soaked with glue.

Repeat on the other siyah.

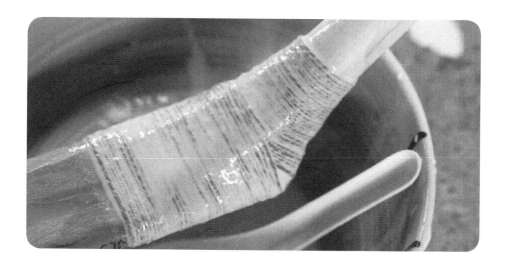

Make sure to soak the wrappings at least twice.

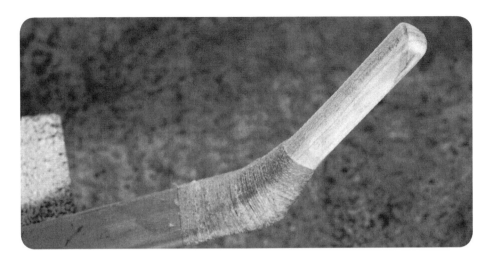

Once both siyahs are soaked, go back to the first one and lightly wipe the siyah down, taking off most of the excess glue.

Do the same to the other siyah.

Place the bow on your drying rack and let both siyahs dry completely.

While the siyahs are drying, get a piece of 3/4 by 3/4 inch piece of wood for the string bridges. Most hardwoods will work, the harder the better. Mark and cut a piece one and a half inches long.

The Impossible Bow

Cut the ends off at roughly a thirty degree angle. You want the smaller side just a little bigger than 3/4 of an inch.

Repeat this for a second piece.

Mark a line on the inside, 1/4 of an inch from the edge.

Cut this inner piece out. An easy way to do this with a coping or scroll saw is to cut straight down to the line, far enough away from the angle for the saw blade to fit.

THE IMPOSSIBLE BOW

Cut along the angle, then tap the wedge with a hammer lightly until it pops off.

Cut down the other angle and along the bottom of the inside until both sides touch.

Make sure both sides are even.

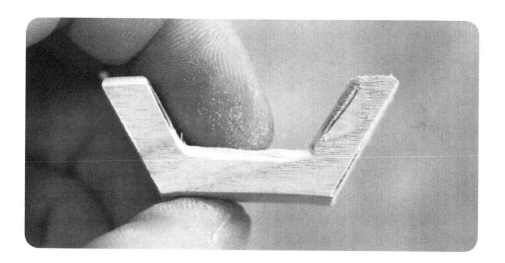

Sand the whole string bridge. The bottom edge should be rounded slightly so it sits on the rounded siyah better.

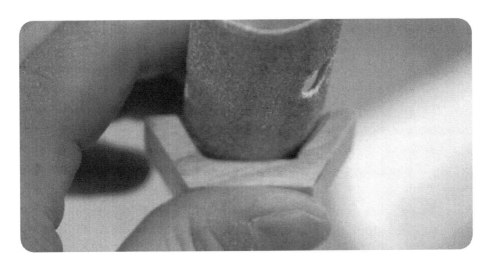

Once the string bridge is sanded, sand the inside bottom with a piece of sandpaper wrapped around a one inch dowel or 3/4 inch PVC pipe.

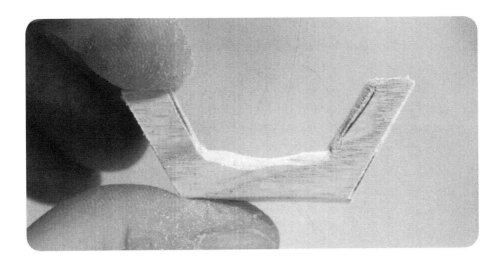

This gives a place for the string to rest and track when the bow is fired. Having the string bridge bowed outward here could result in limb twisting.

Repeat for the other string bridge.

Once the glue is completely dry, measure an inch from the end of the siyah for the nock.

The Impossible Bow

Starting at the one inch mark, file a 1/4 inch deep string nock with a rat tail file. Make sure the bottom of the nock has a bit of a lip to it, so the string does not slip off.

Tie an overhand knot on one side of the string bridge.

Place the string bridge at the base of the siyah like this.

Pull the long end of the cord up and around the siyah.

THE IMPOSSIBLE BOW

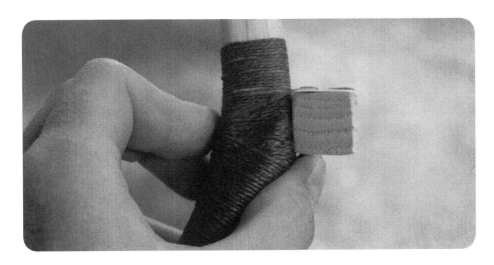

Cross the cord over the back of the siyah, then down into the other end of the string bridge.

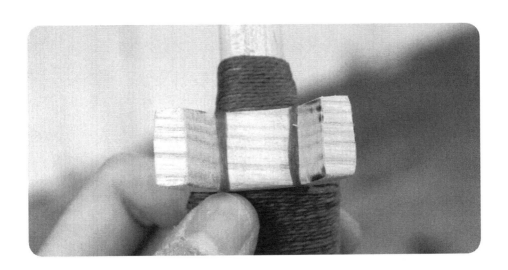

The cords will run on both sides of the string bridge like this.

Bring the cord around, crossing over the back.

Keep crisscrossing the siyah until the string bridge is secure and does not easily move.

Take the loose end of the cord and begin wrapping around the upper part of the siyah.

Wrap about 3/4 of an inch.

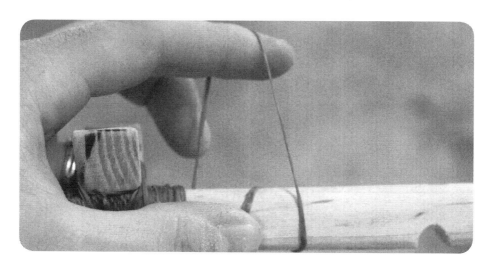

Once the siyah is wrapped, cut the end about ten inches long. Make a loop with the cord, bringing the loose end on the inside, as if you are wrapping backwards.

Unwrap the original wrap you did. If you did the loop right, the wrap will simply be transferred down the siyah. Pull the loose end of the wrap under the original cord.

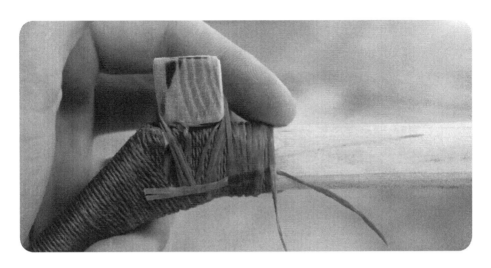

Re-do the original wrap, making sure to keep everything tight.

Pull the loose end through and trim the cord.

Here's the attached string bridge from the belly side.

Repeat the nock and string bridge on the other limb.

The Impossible Bow

Make sure that before you string the bow up for the first time, everything is completely dry. If the wrapping feel wet at all or it still smells like wet glue, let it dry.

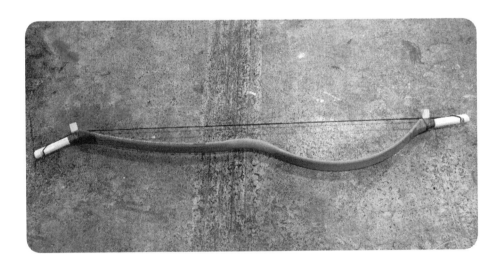

String the bow up. If the limbs were flattened unevenly, this may happen. It could be more drastic or more subtle, depending on how far off you are.

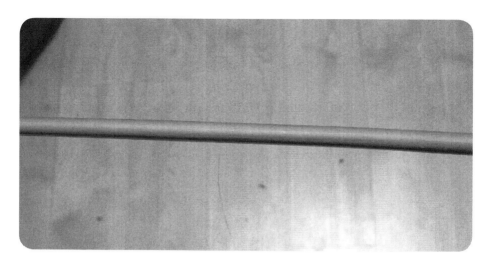

Here's the limb that's not bending as much.

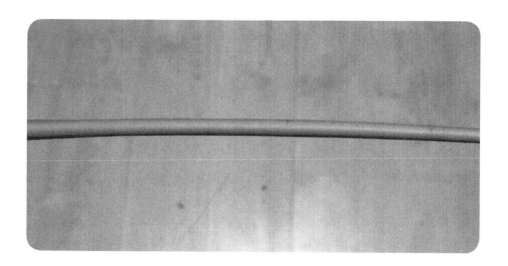

And here is the limb that is bending too much. This is the one we'll be working on first.

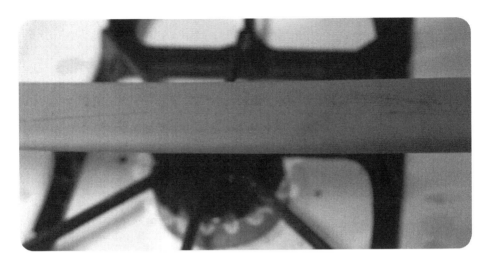

Gently heat the limb up. As the PVC heats up, it will start to puff up and return to its full thickness.

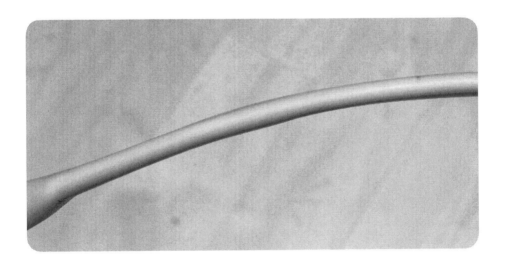

Expand the central part of the limb and also bend the limb slightly.

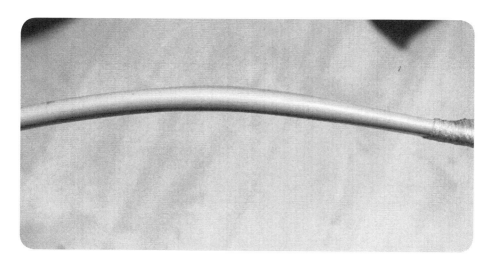

Also expand the area near the siyah, bending slightly.

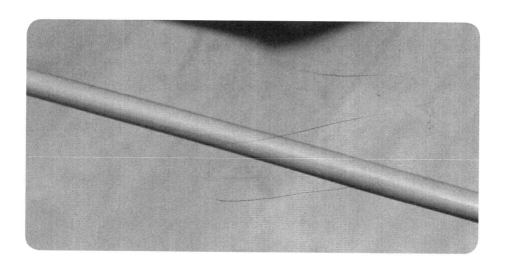

The thicker limb can be thinned if needed, but it's easier to expand the limbs than to compress them.

The Impossible Bow

Heat and bend both limbs until the string bridges and handle touch the ground evenly.

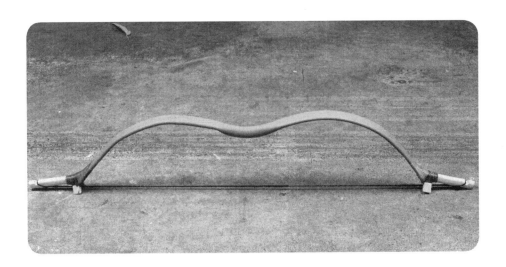

Now string up the bow to full brace. As long as both limbs are fairly even, keep going.

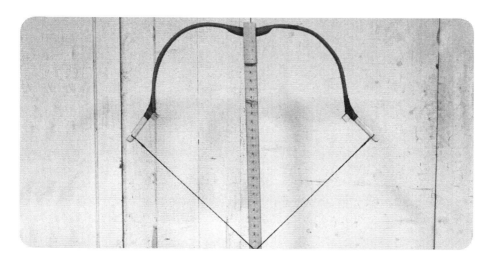

Here's what the bow would look like at full draw now, even with both limbs being uneven. A bow like this is very forgiving, so for now we can go ahead and finish it up before doing the final tiller work.

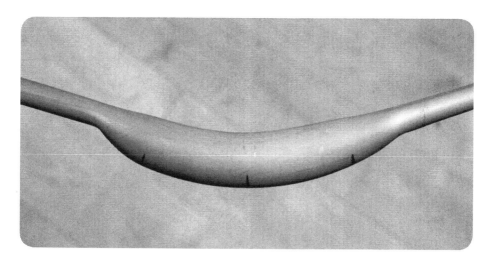

The first thing we need to do (before pulling the bow to full draw) is take out the sharp corners in the handle.

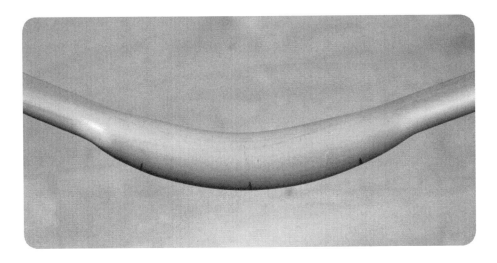

Heat the areas right near the handle where it goes into the bow limbs. Let these puff up a little so that the transition from handle to limb is smooth. This will prevent any collapses or bending in this area.

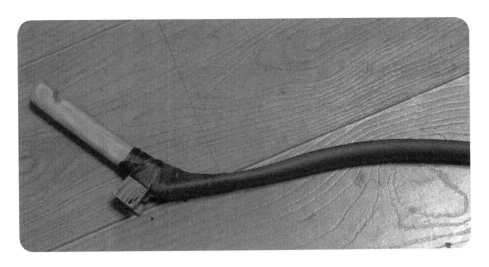

Heat the area just beyond the wrapping on the siyah and bend it forward slightly.

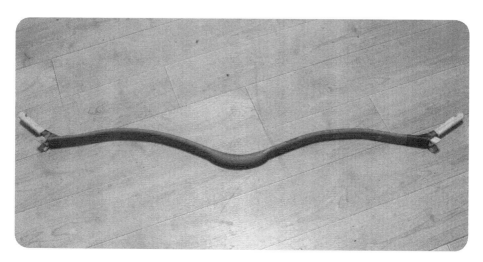

This is what the bow should look like now. It is ready to be covered up and finished. If you plan on putting on a permanent finish like paint, glued on leather, paper, etc., or anything else that can't be easily removed like tape, I suggest just wrapping the bow in plain duct tape for now.

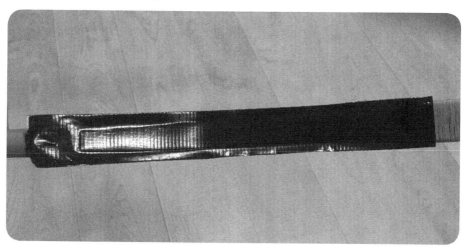

The reason for this is that the bow still needs to be finish-tillered, but it should be protected from sunlight before shooting it out, as the strain on the limbs combined with sun could cause the bow to break early. If finishing in duct tape, start by placing one strip from where the siyahs end to the handle.

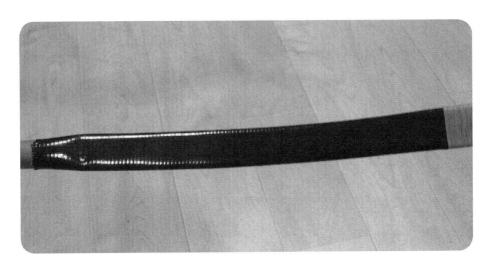

Smooth the duct tape over.

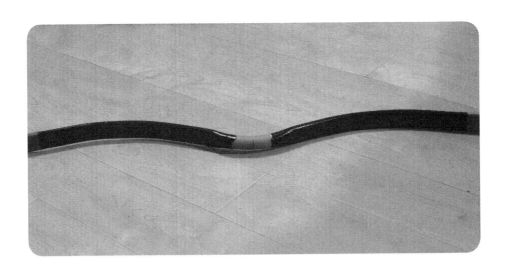

Repeat on both sides. Black duct tape gives the effect of a horn belly at a distance, which is why I will often use it on the belly and glue hide or patterned cloth on the back of the bow.

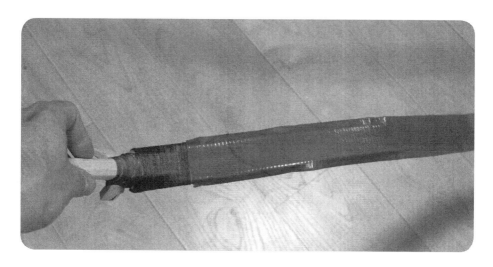

Start the top layer of duct tape at the base of the wrapping of one siyah. Even if you plan on wrapping or painting, a layer of UV-resistant duct tape can give you a little extra insurance against UV damage.

Continue the tape down to the other siyah.

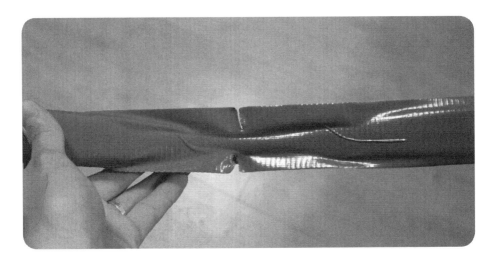

Cut the tape near the handle and smooth it down the entire bow. You could also use two strips instead of one.

Trim the tape at the end where the siyah wrap starts.

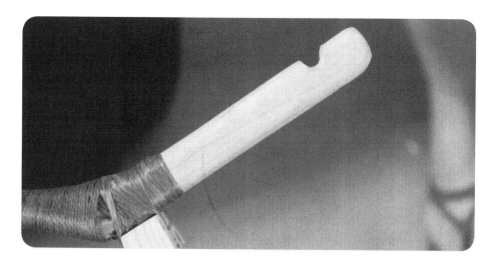

The next thing to do is finish up the exposed parts of the siyahs.

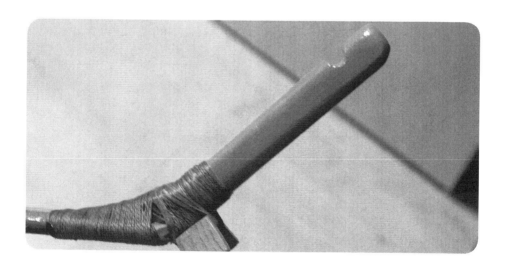

I like to apply a waterproof paint on all the wood parts. Exterior house paint works very well.

Wipe the siyah clean with a damp rag to leave a nice, stained look. This can be finished with clear coat over the entire siyah. You can also let the paint dry.

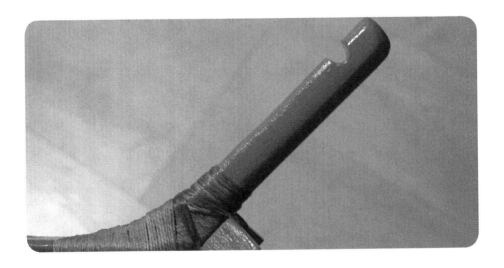

Repeat on the other siyah.

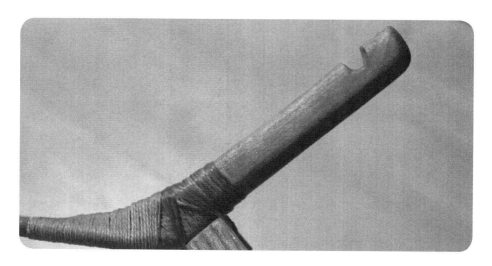

Any other stain or finish of choice can be applied. Use your imagination.

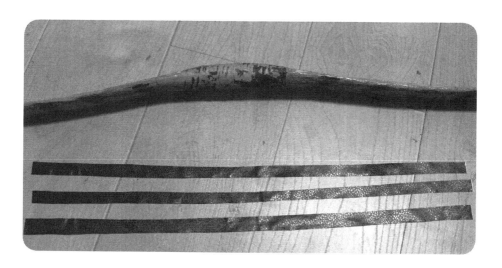

Next we'll be covering the handle. This bow is based on a short bow from Mongolia. On the antique bow, the handle is a wrap of overlapping birch bark strips. Here, we will use imitation leather. Any thin leather or vinyl will work for the job.

THE IMPOSSIBLE BOW

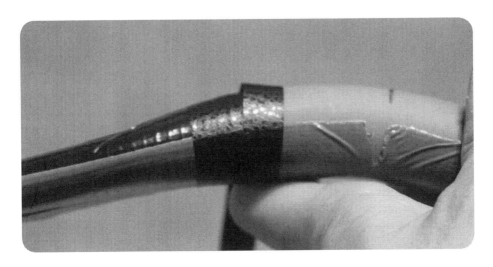

Start by wrapping the vinyl in place. If using non-adhesive vinyl or leather, contact cement works well.

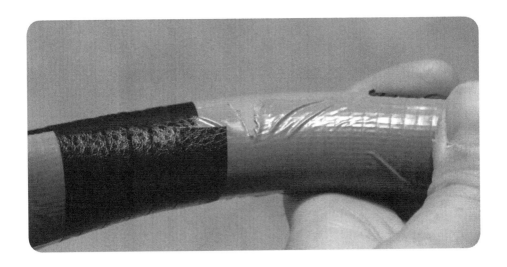

Keep wrapping until the strip ends.

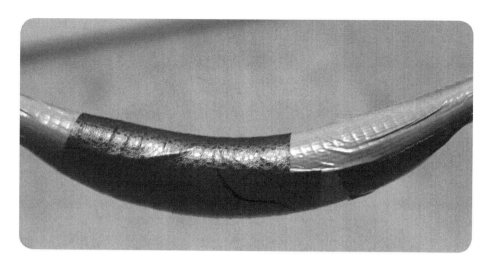

Continue with the next strip.

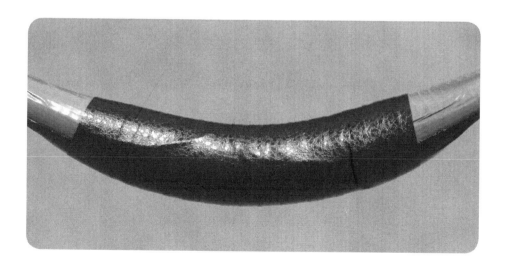

Then finish up with the last strip, completing the handle.

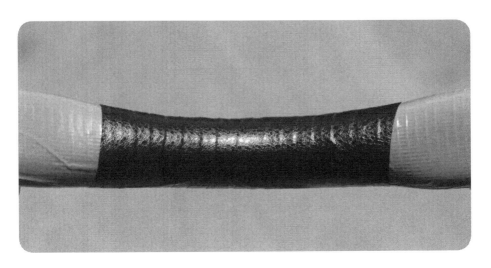

Here's the wrap from the back of the bow.

From the belly.

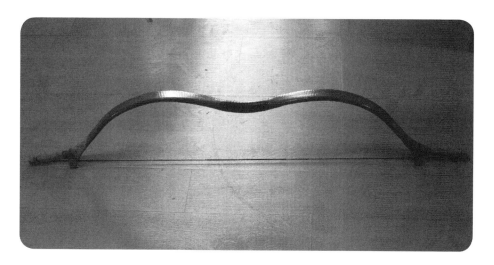

Once finished, string the bow up to full brace.

Here it is at full draw. With a very short bow like this, it is hard to find any flaws until they start to present themselves, so shoot the bow out until anything shows up.

Finishing

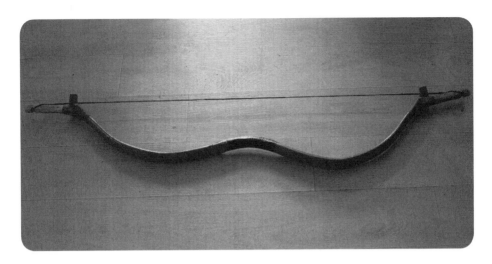

This is a good example of what can happen. If one limb is too weak, the plastic can collapse. If the limbs look uneven like this, do not shoot the bow further.

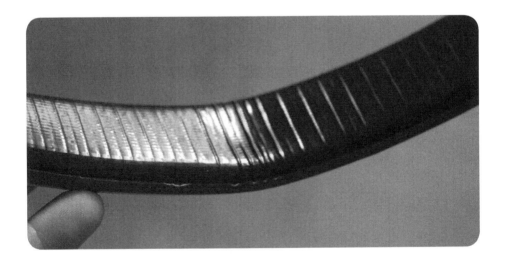

Most times, a sharp crease will form.

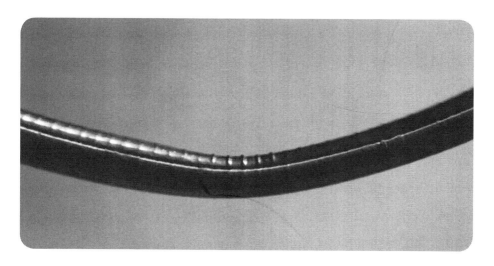

From the side, you can see where the plastic is pinched and weakened.

Take your collapsed limb over your heat source, gently heating it up. The plastic will heat through the duct tape, just do not get it too close as it may burn or melt.

THE IMPOSSIBLE BOW

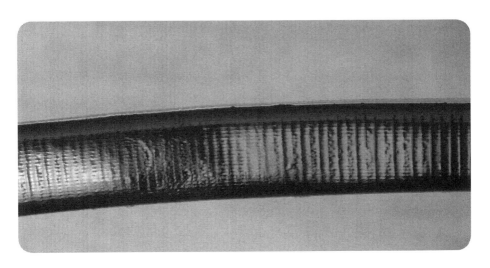

Once the limb heats up enough, the bow will start to puff up in the affected area. With an oven mitt or heat resistant pad, hold the limb until it sets.

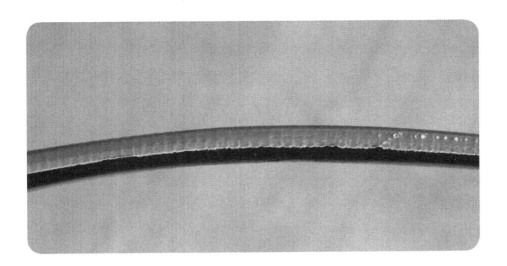

From the side, here is the repair.

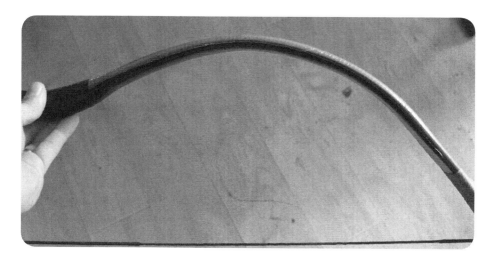

Once cooled either in air or under running water, the limb should bend evenly when at full brace.

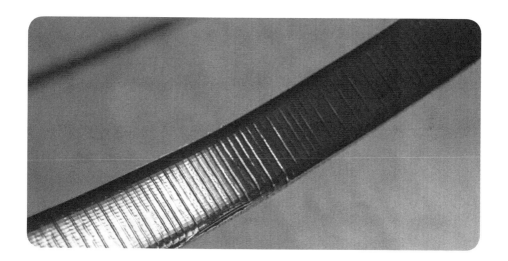

See how the affected area is no longer smashed or pinched.

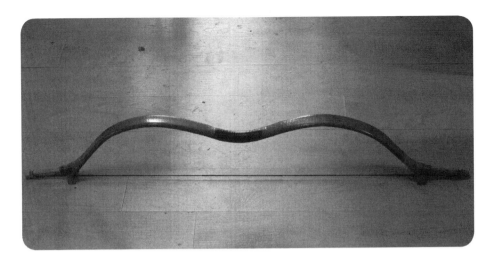

Now it is time to fine-tune the brace. Adjust the string until the braced string just rests on the string bridges. Measure the brace height.

Now heat the handle up where it was bent the first time.

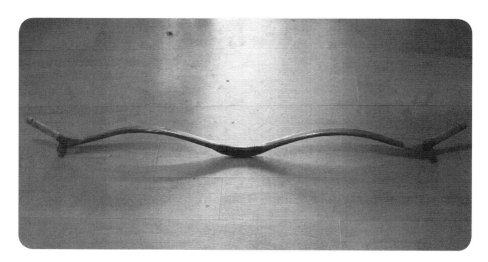

Take your brace height measurement and subtract it from six. Take this number and flex the handle towards the back until the bow's tips move that far. Basically, if the brace height is four inches, then flex the handle towards the belly until the tips move two inches towards the belly.

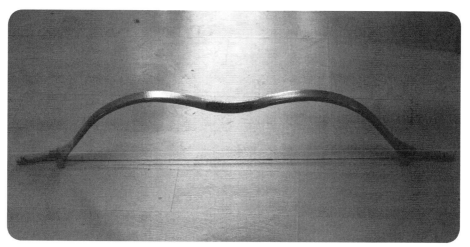

Now when the bow is braced, the brace height will be six inches and the string will rest on the string bridges. This will also take extra stress from the limbs.

THE IMPOSSIBLE BOW

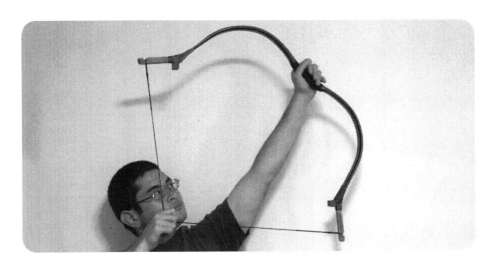

Once everything is cooled, give the bow a few test pulls.

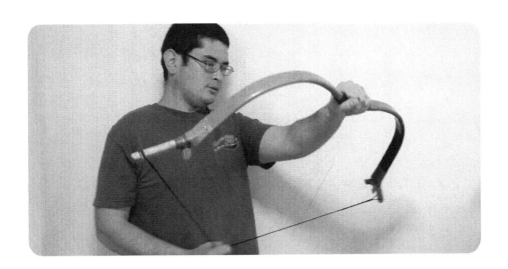

Make sure that everything lines up and that the bow bends evenly.

Correcting Tillering Errors

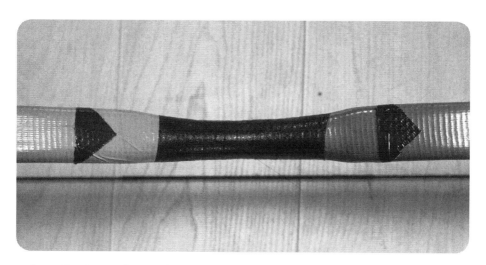

As a final touch, mark the top limb. This limb will be the one that bends more than the other. The reason for this is that when the arrow is placed on the bow, the lower limb will have to bend more than the top. So putting the weaker limb on top evens this out.

Now your new bow is ready to shoot! The bow should now be solid and dependable. It's a great little bow, and is well-suited for the beginning horse-archer.

CHAPTER FIVE -
EXTRA EQUIPMENT

Now that you have a bow, the next step is to go out and shoot. If you are anything like how I used to be, it takes a lot to get out and shooting. Having an easy to use quiver and a target in my backyard makes practice easy. As long as I can simply go outside, shoot a few arrows, and continue my day without having to mess with things, I get good practice in.

This chapter is all about making simple equipment to make archery in your backyard a little more enjoyable. We will be building two very simple quivers to hold your arrows. These are about as basic as they get, but they work well. We will also go over making a thumb ring to protect your thumb when drawing with the Mongolian release, as well as making a simple target stand and targets for your backyard, hallway, or garage.

Quivers

No foray into the backyard or to the range would be complete without a quiver for your arrows. And of course, if you're shooting a PVC bow, your quiver has to made of PVC as well. While they are a little heavy, they make great little quivers, and with a little fur or soft lining, they can make good hunting quivers.

The first quiver is a small one, great for up to six arrows. This one is a good quiver for the target range, and can be carried on a belt, across the shoulder, under the arm, off to the side, and like a backpack. It's also PVC, so it's tough. I've run over one before and it saved my arrows from a certain doom.

The second quiver is larger, good for about twelve arrows or about ten with broadheads. It is my preferred quiver for hunting, slung over my shoulder with a fur lining and leather straps. It can be carried like the other quiver, but is a little big, so over the shoulder and on the back are the easiest ways to carry it.

Because PVC is heavy, these can be made with foam core ABS plastic pipe, which will dramatically cut the weight of the quiver. This is important for hunting, hiking, and even a day at the range. As for finishing, nothing is wrong with duct tape, cord-wrapping, or even just painting. Use your imagination! PVC can also make a good inner tube for soft leather or cloth quivers.

THE IMPOSSIBLE BOW

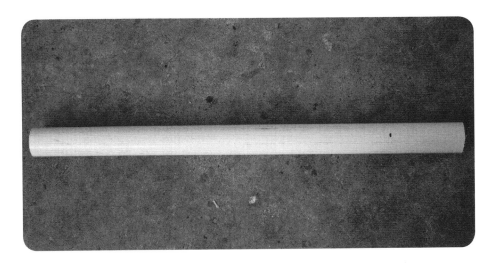

Start with a two foot length of 1 1/4" pipe.

Mark four inches in from the end of the pipe.

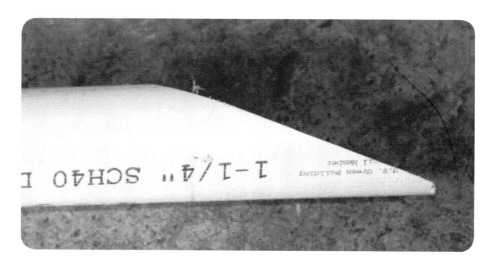

Cut in a straight line from the end of the pipe to the mark on the opposite side.

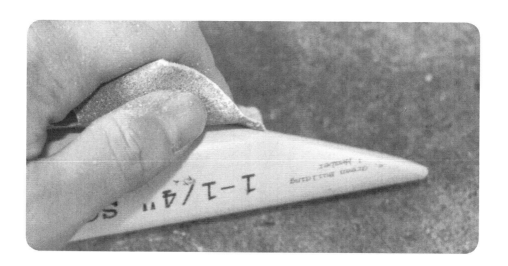

Clean up this edge and round it off.

THE IMPOSSIBLE BOW

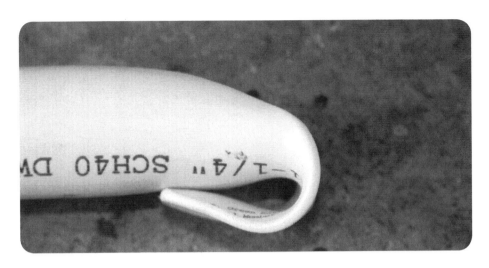

Heat the end of the pipe, then bend the tip back until it reaches about halfway to the four inch mark.

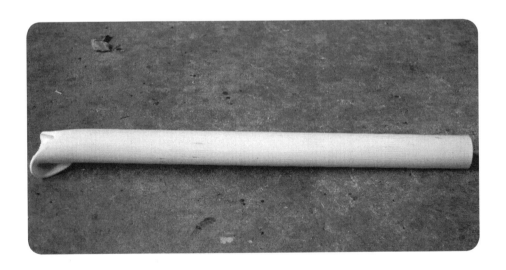

Here is the quiver at this point. Keep the quiver on the ground like this, as the next step will be done from this position.

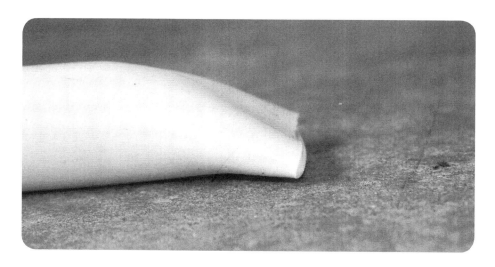

Flatten the end of the pipe about two to three inches in.

Drill two holes at the bottom of the flattened pipe.

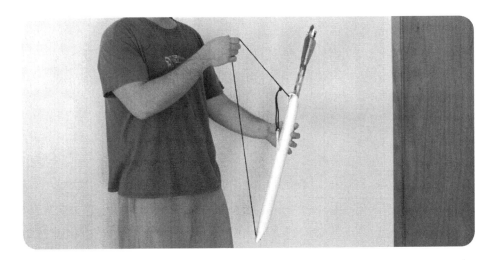

String a length of rope from the bottom holes and through the top loop, forming a strap for the quiver. This will vary in length depending on how you want the quiver to hang.

It can be slung across the shoulder.

To take out an arrow, simply reach across the back and grip the nock end of the arrow.

Pull the arrow out. The quiver should be just high enough so you can easily pull out an arrow and don't need to stretch.

THE IMPOSSIBLE BOW

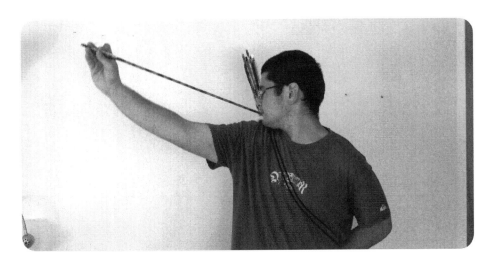

To put an arrow back, reach back with your other hand and lift the bottom of the quiver. Then place the tip of the arrow upon the rounded edge of the quiver.

The arrow can then be slid in easily.

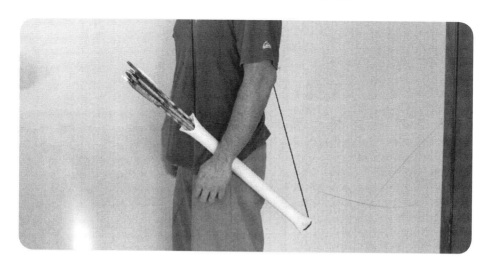

The quiver an also be held at the side.

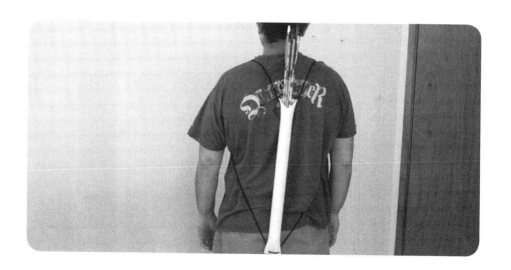

And you can also wear it on the back like a backpack.

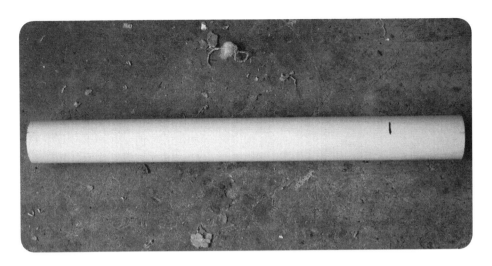

To make a larger quiver, start with a two inch diameter pipe, two feet long. Mark four inches in from the end of the pipe.

Cut from the end of the pipe to the four inch mark in a straight line.

Sand and round the edges of the pipe.

Here's the pipe after cleaning the end.

THE IMPOSSIBLE BOW

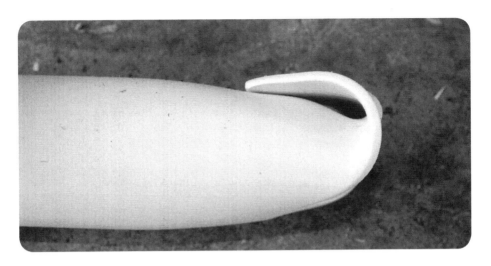

Heat and bend the end of the pipe back onto the main body of pipe, back until the four inch mark, so two inches back.

The end should look flattened like this.

Flatten the bottom of the pipe and drill two holes.

Here is the finished quiver.

THE IMPOSSIBLE BOW

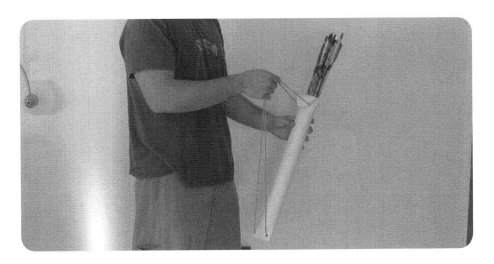

A length of rope completes the quiver as a strap.

Slung across the shoulder, this makes a great quiver.

To retrieve an arrow, simply reach back and grasp an arrow by the nock.

Pull the arrow out and you are ready to shoot.

THE IMPOSSIBLE BOW

To put the arrow back, simply lift the quiver with your off hand and place the arrow back. This can be done with a bow in the hand.

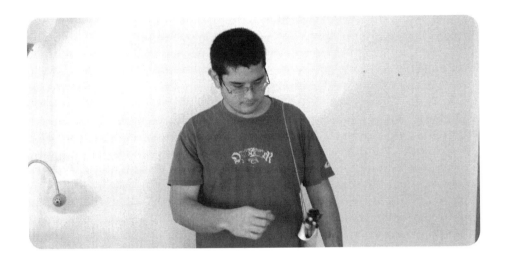

You can also wear the quiver on the side or more like a backpack.

THUMB RING

In many parts of the world where short composite bows were used, drawing the bow with the thumb instead of the first three fingers was favored. In most cases, the thumb draw allowed short bows to be released cleanly, as the angle of the string at the arrow nock is much more acute when the bow is short.

The thumb draw, also known as the Mongolian draw or Mongolian release, is a great way to draw a bow. If you try to shoot most of the bows in this book with the "standard" Mediterranean three finger release, you will know what string pinch is. Not only can it be painful, but it also can make getting a clean release almost impossible.

If practiced regularly, the Mongolian release can also alleviate shoulder strain. Much like a modern mechanical release, the thumb draw places your palm down. This is a much more natural and ergonomic position of your arm as opposed to the palm facing inward, like the three finger draw. Once your thumb grows used to it, even heavy bows can be drawn with less fatigue and wear on your joints.

While the Mongolian draw is easy on your joints, it can be very hard on your thumb. The three finger release distributes the pressure of the string evenly across three fingers, so the string does not cut into the fingers too much. With the Mongolian draw, the thumb takes all the force of the string, and on shorter bows, the string almost wraps around the base of the thumb. This can cause numbness, blood vessel constriction, and a host of other painful problems if the thumb is either not protected or not used to drawing a bow.

Traditionally, this problem is remedied through the use of either a leather pad for the thumb, or a thumb ring. The thumb ring can range in design from a simple band to a lever-like device which fully cups the pad of the thumb and a place for the string to rest

The Impossible Bow

while the bow is drawn. Thumb rings can be made of bone, horn, hardened leather, stone, metal, wood, and nowadays even plastic.

This thumb ring is made of PVC, and with a little bit of shaping and forming, a very comfortable and snug-fitting thumb ring can be made. This particular design is good for starting out with the Mongolian draw. It has full coverage on the pad of the thumb as well as a slot for the string to sit while the bow is drawn.

Either gray or white PVC will work for this thumb ring. In order to find the size of pipe you will need, try and push your thumb into the end of your pipe. If it slides in easily, go one size smaller. If the 1/2 inch pie slides on easily as well, the pipe can be heated and made to fit, but it is easier to stretch small pipe than to compress it if it's too large.

With that said, let's get started!

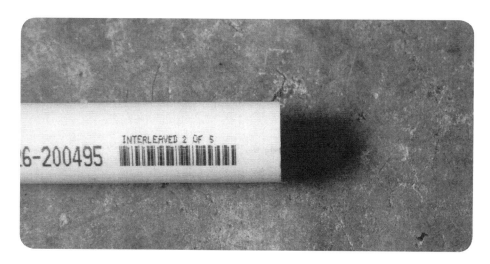

Start out with some PVC pipe. The diameter of the pipe depends on the size of your thumb. Try to fit your thumb into the pipe. If it fits easily, go smaller. If it does not fit, try a larger pipe. If it fits easily in the larger pipe, go back to the smaller pipe.

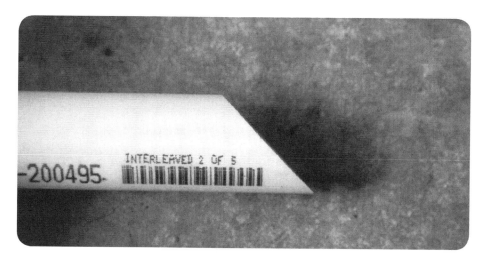

Cut a forty-five degree angle in the pipe. Your thumb should now fit in the opening of the pipe somewhat. If it doesn't the pipe will have to be stretched a bit.

The Impossible Bow

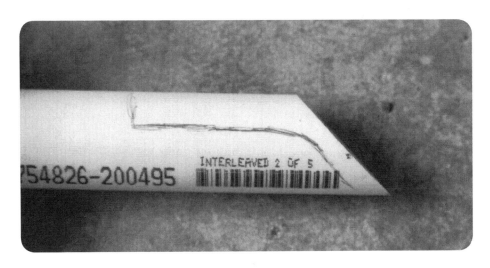

Draw a line that follows the angled cut, 1/4 of an inch wide, then widens to 3/8 of an inch for one and a half inches.

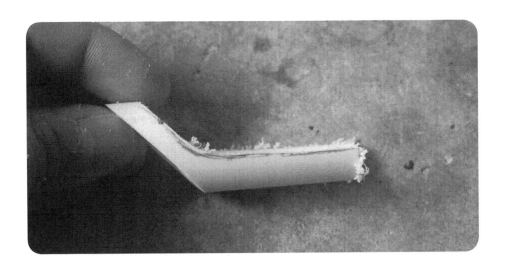

Cut along the line, freeing the thumb ring blank from the rest of the pipe.

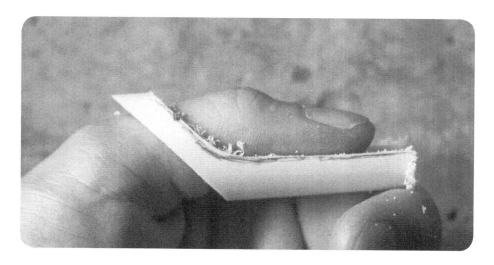

Test fit the ring on your thumb. If the ring is too loose, you may have to go smaller. If you are already using 1/2 an inch pipe, it will need to be compressed later.

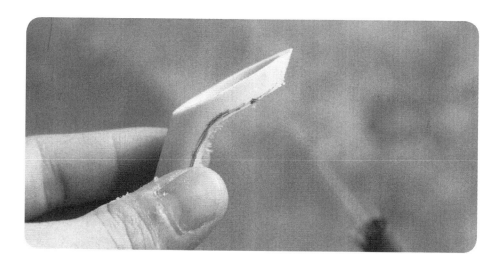

With a torch or other heat source, heat the back of the ring's band.

THE IMPOSSIBLE BOW

Heat it from both sides, so that it will bend evenly.

Bend the band down until the end comes back down about halfway.

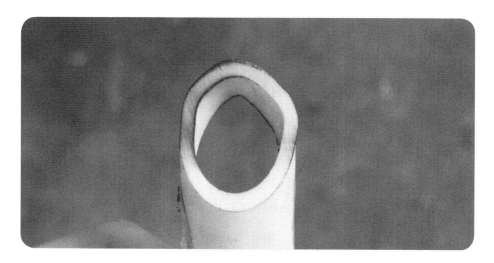

The pipe may be a little looser now, so press in the sides a little, making the opening smaller near the back.

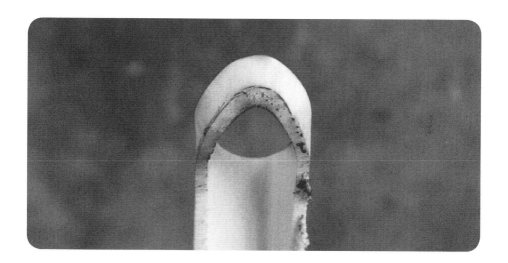

Make sure the band is still straight, and not smashed to one side or extremely crooked.

THE IMPOSSIBLE BOW

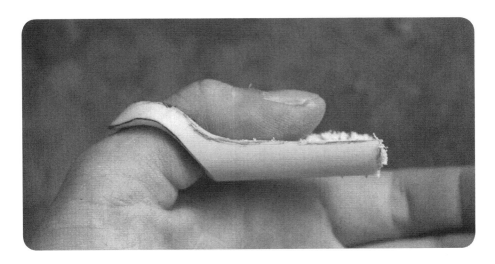

Test fit the ring. Your thumb should fit easily inside sideways, but when resting along the inside of the ring, the band should lock against the back of the first joint.

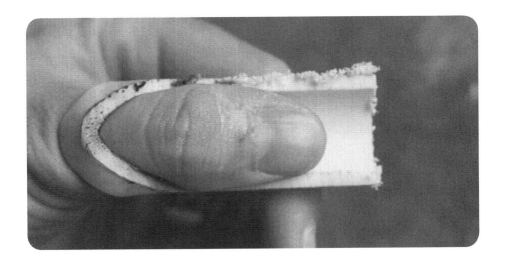

Here's what it should look like from the top. With a pen, mark around your thumb, as we will be cutting the end away.

With a saw, sander, or file, cut the pad of the ring around where you marked.

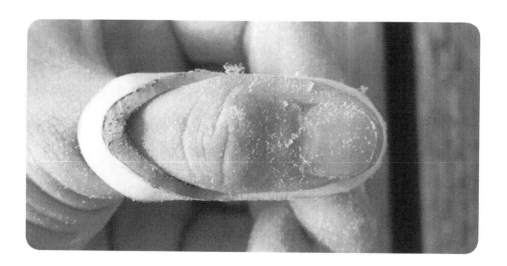

There should only be a thin line of pipe showing around your thumb now.

THE IMPOSSIBLE BOW

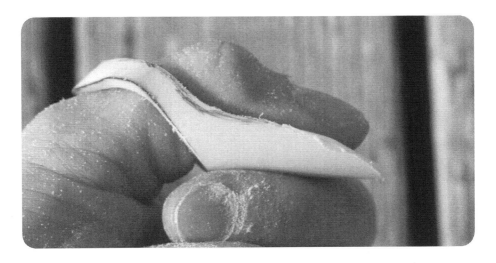

Here is how the ring should be fitting now. Keep note of where your thumb naturally curves up toward the nail.

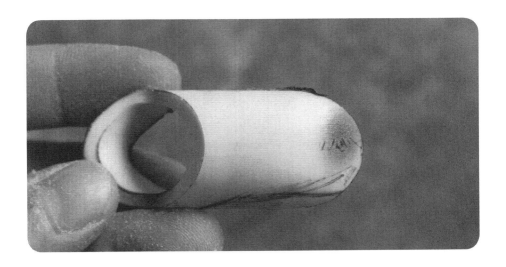

Next, heat the front of the pad, right around where that curve of your thumb should be.

Press the front edge up into a spoon-like shape. This shape can be obtained by actually pressing the heated pipe into the bowl of a teaspoon until it sets.

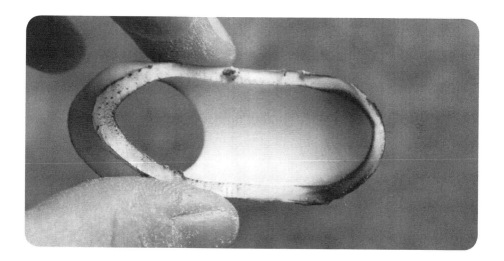

Here's the ring from the top.

The Impossible Bow

Here it is from the front. The pad does not need to be completely even at this point, as we will be sanding and cleaning up the edges later.

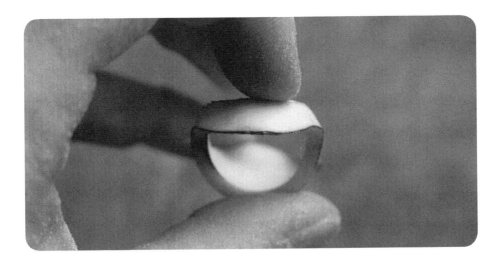

Here's the ring from the back.

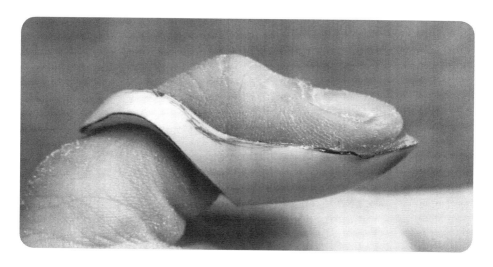

Your thumb should fit snugly into the pad of the ring, as if the ring is now part of your thumb.

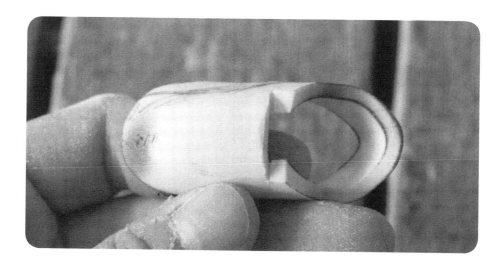

Next, file a groove about 1/8 of an inch in and about 1/8 of an inch deep into the ring, just behind the pad of the thumb. This will hold the string in place when the bow is drawn.

The Impossible Bow

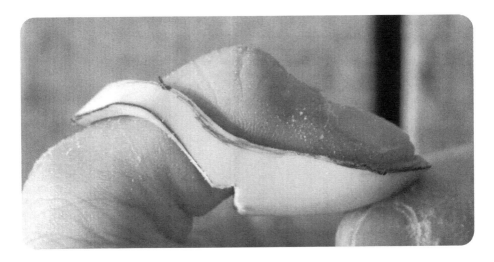

Test fit the ring one more time. The first joint of the thumb should lock the ring into place, keeping if from being pulled straight off your thumb.

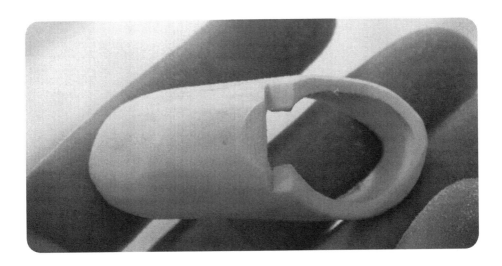

With a file or belt sander, smooth the outside of the ring and even up the edges. Also round the string groove so that the string can come out of it without catching on the square edge.

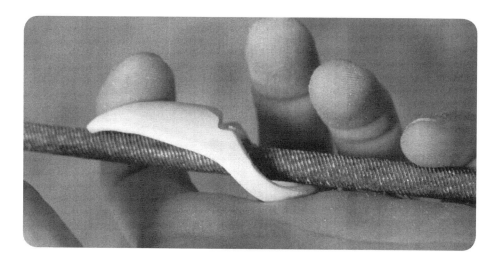

With a round file or sandpaper, clean out the inside of the ring. Also round off the inside of the band so that it does not cut into your thumb. All sharp edges should be smoothed down.

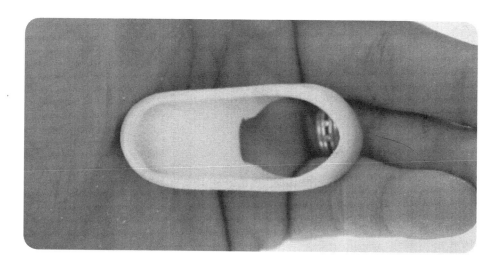

Once the inside is cleaned up, sand to at least four hundred grit sandpaper, A light buffing on a wheel or with a soft cloth can be used to bring the plastic to a light polish. Next are some pictures of the finished ring from all sides. Here it is from the top.

THE IMPOSSIBLE BOW

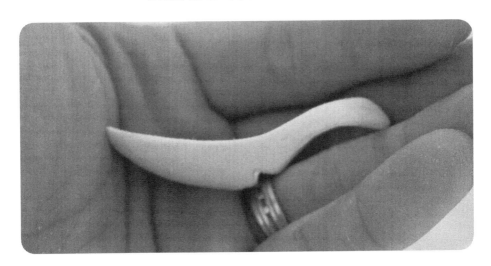

The side.

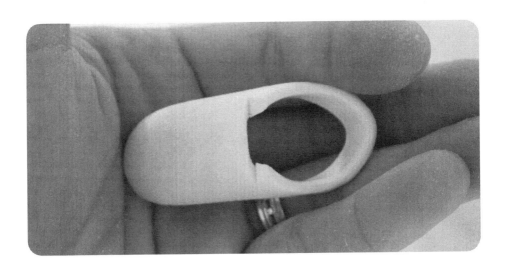

The top, angled to see the inside of the band.

Thumb Ring

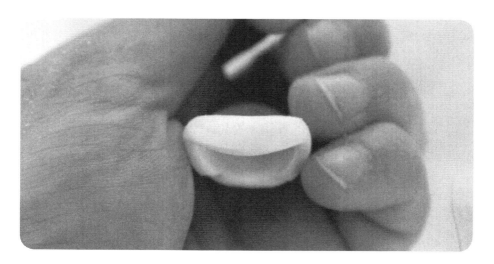

The back.

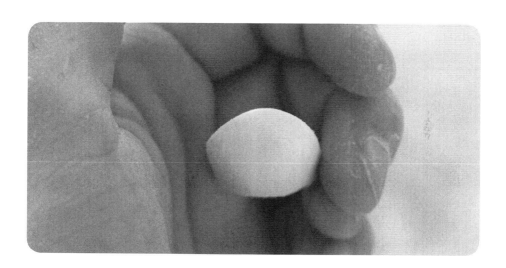

The front.

THE IMPOSSIBLE BOW

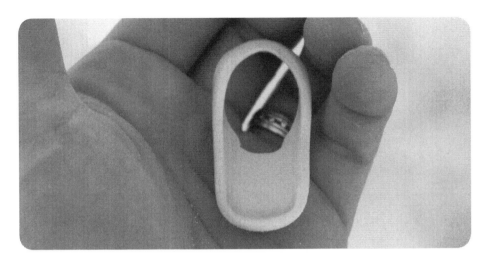

The bottom.

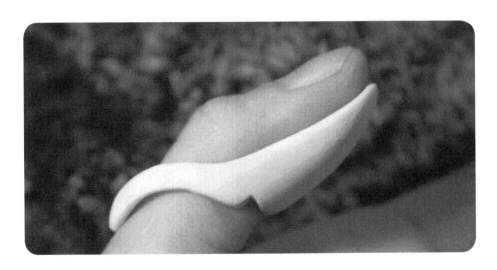

Finally, here is the finished ring from the side, showing how it should fit on your thumb. Enjoy your new thumb ring! You may have to make another one once you get a hang of the thumb release, as you start finding out what feels best for you.

NICHOLAS TOMIHAMA

TARGET

No backyard archery setup would be complete without a target. While there are many types of targets available, and many other that can be made easily, this particular one can be made with pillows, plastic bags, and PVC pipe. What's great is that any of these can be substituted for whatever you have on hand.

This target is intended for use in front of a solid stop of some sort. Usually 1/2 an inch to 1 inch plywood makes a decent stop, or at least make sure there is a good amount of open space behind the target. A solid wall behind the target will work as well, but be careful, as doing this may destroy arrows quickly. If you have a large old rug and a place to hang it, it will help stop arrows that miss the target.

I like this target because it can be taken down easily and stored out of the way. It is also much easier to get into a car than most large foam or sack targets. If you do prefer a larger, fixed target one can be made by taking a stack of material and binding it like a hay bale. Cardboard, carpets, foam mats, and even bales of hay make great targets. Any of those things can also be used as filling in this target as well, though hay may not stop arrows if it is packed loosely into the bag.

The Impossible Bow

Start with six, four foot long pieces of PVC pipe (any size) and four elbow connectors. This is for your target stand. This stand can be used for any hanging targets.

Mark one foot up from the bottom of each leg.

Drill a hole just large enough for a length of rope to pass through.

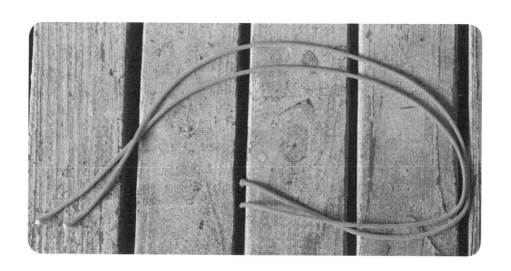

Cut two pieces of rope, preferably parachute cord or something similar, two feet long.

THE IMPOSSIBLE BOW

Tie an overhand knot three inches in from the end of both lengths of rope.

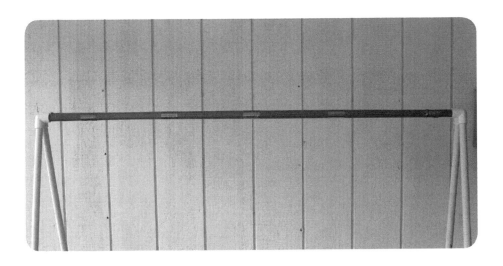

Assemble the PVC pipes into two square frames (with the bottom open), and tape or tie the two frames together.

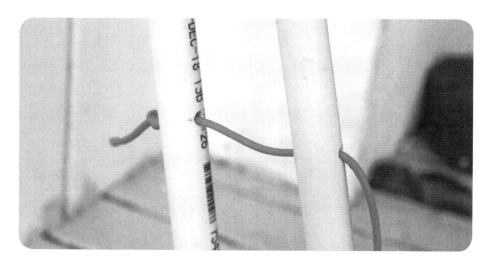

Run the rope through two of the legs, letting the knot stop the cord form going in all the way.

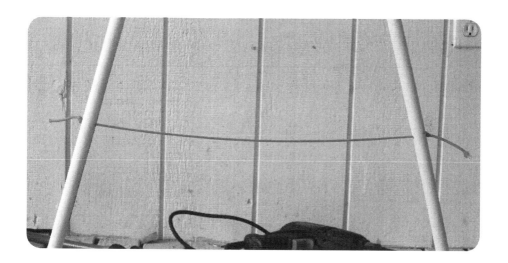

Tie the other knot at three inches, then open the two halves of the stand. This will keep the stand from falling over. Your stand is complete.

The Impossible Bow

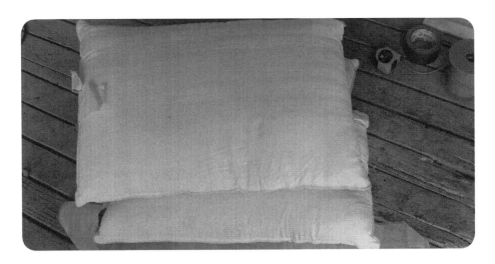

Now we will prepare a basic target. Around three full size pillows, a stack of cardboard at least ten inches thick, or enough rags to pack fully into the bag you will use will work for target filling.

Place your target filling into a bag. I am using a trash bag here, but almost any other type of bag or sack will work. If you can find some old burlap sacks, these will work better in the long run, allowing you to patch over the center when it gets shot out. Plastic bags can be wasteful and expensive.

Simply tie your target to the stand, and you are ready to go. You could either hang a larger target (up to four feet by four feet) or two or more smaller targets. A run can also be hung over the back of the target to keep stray arrows from getting past your target.

Most filling will stop an arrow without any problems. The lowest arrow in the right target was fired from a seventy pound compound bow, and it didn't make it through the target.

CHAPTER SIX -
USING AND CARING FOR
YOUR BOW

Your PVC bow can be dependable and last for a long time if cared for properly. If treated like a real bow, PVC has the ability to work fairly well. If treated like it is not a real bow, and therefore without respect, do not expect it to last or work well for you.

In this chapter, we'll go over one way to string your new bow safely. We will also go over how to shoot using the Mongolian Draw, which is an effective way of shooting very short bows like the one in this book. It is also a great way to avoid excess strain on your shoulder and string slap on your wrist and forearm.

We will also go over the many causes and signs of bow failure. We will go over the different causes, what can be done to identify the causes, and any possible fixes or remedies. This last section will also go over how long a bow may last, as well as tips on making them last.

NICHOLAS TOMIHAMA

STRINGING THE BOW

One of the simplest way to care for your bow is to string it properly. There are a variety of ways to safely string a bow (some of the safest actually require two or more people). Of them, a device known as a bow stringer is perhaps the safest for a person to do by themselves. The problem with a bow stringer is that they don't work as well will PVC bows, and glued on siyahs may break if pulled back with a bow stringer.

This is not the best way to string a bow, but it is safe and fairly easy to do. It is especially well-suited for bows with heavy recurved tips and glued on siyahs, as most of the pressure can be directed to the limbs behind the tips, rather than on the tips themselves.

I also find that this method of stringing a bow works for even very heavy bows, and you can use your own body as leverage to flex the bow. The only trick to this method is learning to flex both limbs equally. It is easy to actually lock the lower limb with your leg, and then force the upper limb to bend too far, causing uneven bending, and sometimes even a broken bow.

I suggest practicing this method a few times before actually stringing up a bow, getting used to how it feels. Never string or unstring a bow by pushing down on the top limb, driving the lower limb into the ground and potentially ruining the nocks and causing limb twist. It is also easy to break wooden siyahs with this method.

With that said, let me show you how I string my bows.

The Impossible Bow

Start out by holding your bow with your dominant hand, just below any recurves or about eight inches below the nock.

Holding the bow with your dominant hand and the string in your other hand, rest the other end of the bow on your shin, either below any recurves or eight inches from the end. Step over the bow with your dominant side leg.

Stringing the Bow

Bend your dominant side knee a little, pressing into the handle of the bow.

Continue bending your knee, then bring your dominant hand forward, causing the bow to flex to its braced level. Bring the string loop over, and slip it over the nock of the bow.

Stringing the Bow

THE IMPOSSIBLE BOW

Step out of the bow, and viola! Your bow is now strung. To unstring the bow, just do everything in reverse.

Here are the steps over again, just up close so you can see what is going on easier.

Stringing the Bow

Make sure the lower limb of the bow rests on your leg behind the recurve or siyah. If you rest the siyah on your leg, you have a good chance of snapping it off.

When bringing the string up, make sure that the string is still secure in the loop. Also make that if there are any string bridges or string grooves, the string is aligned in them.

Here you can more or less see that the bow is flexing evenly. It is easy to bend one limb more than the other, so just be mindful of it. Your leg and arm should be holding the same amount of pressure. When slipping the loop over the nock, resist the urge to push directly on the top siyah, as this too may weaken or snap it.

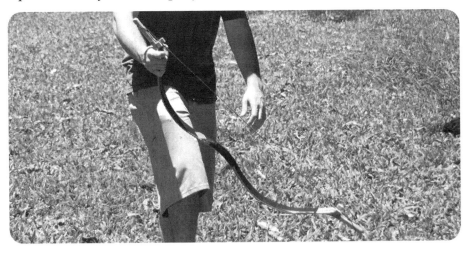

Here's the bow, strung and ready to go.

Nicholas Tomihama

The Mongolian Draw

True to its name, the Mongolian draw was used by the steppe nomads collectively known as the Mongols, and even today in Mongolia (though the three finger draw and modified thumb draw is quite popular nowadays). The Mongolian or thumb draw is quite common in many places in Asia, and modified thumb draws are used all over the world.

Like I said in the section on making a thumb ring, the Mongolian draw is a great style of shooting, and if practiced regularly, can be as reliable if not more so than the three finger Mediterranean draw. I use this draw regularly, but if I don't have a thumb ring on me, I use the three finger draw for test-drawing heavier weight bows when I build them.

The thumb draw is very good for your body. I am still very young, but ever since I started archery I was always plagued by a constant pain in my right shoulder. It was bad, and no matter how much I practiced with a bow or gave it rest, it was still there. It was such a problem for me that my first book was delayed because the pain in my shoulder made holding a pen or typing on a keyboard an arduous and excruciating task.

That was, until I found the thumb draw. It was awkward at first, especially because I am right handed, and shot a right handed bow. The transition to a left handed bow was odd, as the easiest way to use the thumb draw is by shooting the arrow off the side of the bow away from your body. For a long time I kept planting arrows into lamp poles and target frames because I had a hard time learning a new point of reference.

Yet I kept going, and after a few weeks, I noticed for the first time that my shoulder pain was gone. It may have taken a while to notice because during those first few weeks, my thumb alternated between pain and just feeling swollen. After the pain in my thumb went away, I found that I could start drawing heavier weights

The Impossible Bow

without hurting my shoulder as much.

I also found that this release gave me much more leeway as far as how I held my bow. With the three finger release, I found myself having to cant my bow over to the right to prevent the arrow from falling off the bow. It got to the point that now I cant the bow out of habit, even on bows with captive rests or centered arrow shelves. Once I got a hang of the thumb draw, I found that contrary to my first impressions, I did not need to cant the bow to the left.

Due to the torque on the string by my thumb, as well as the arrow being stuck in place by my drawing hand and the bow, I don't have to worry about the arrow just falling off. I can hold the bow vertical, horizontal, and even canted to the right (which is what have a habit of doing) without the arrow falling or slipping around. I even have less problems with nocks that don't lock onto the string than with the three finger draw.

There is also another side-effect of this draw that has enamored me even more. I used to use an arm guard, but got tired of using after some time, just holding my bow arm in such a way that I avoided hitting my arm. I still used the guard from time to time, as sometimes the string would hit my bare arm, causing the arrow to fly wild. Now that is something an arm guard really helps with. With the thumb draw, wrist slap is very rare, and for the most part an arm guard is not needed.

This draw is also great as it gives you the ability to shoot left handed bows if you are right handed, and vice-versa for lefties. Another thing to keep in mind is that the thumb draw can increase your draw length by an inch or two if you anchor your hand in the same spot as a three finger draw.

Start by nocking the arrow onto the bow, on the side of the bow that faces away from your bow holding arm.

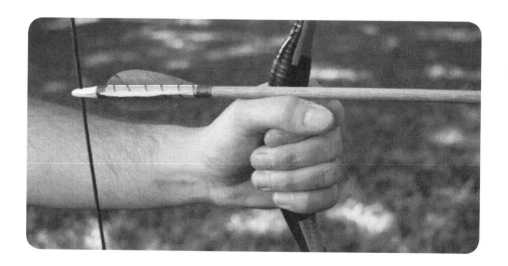

Here it is up close. If you were shooting three fingers, this would be the wrong side of the bow. If you are shooting without an arrow rest, the arrow will rest on your thumb.

The Impossible Bow

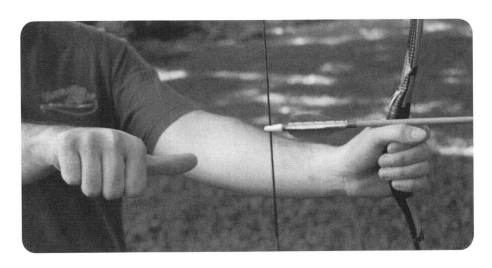

Take your drawing hand, make a fist, the stick your thumb straight out, like the classic hitch hiker's gesture.

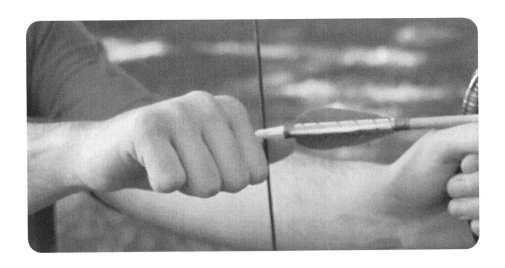

Place your thumb onto the string just below the arrow, resting the string in the first joint.

The Mongolian Draw

Close your thumb over the string, making sure the arrow nock is resting on top of your thumb.

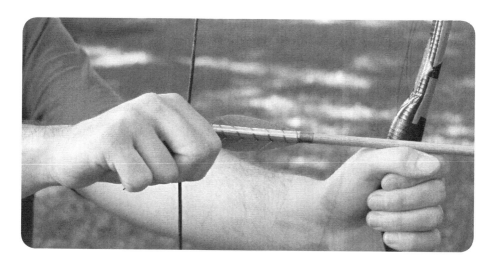

Slip your first two fingers over your thumb, and try to keep a closed fist. These two fingers will assist the thumb during the draw, and will be doing the pulling. Your thumb is mainly serving as a lever that holds the string in place.

The Impossible Bow

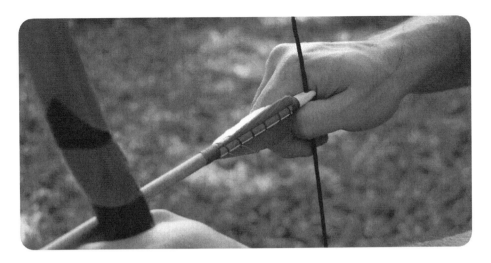

From the other side, you can see that your fist creates a sort of closed triangle that cradles the end of the arrow. By pushing in with your fist ever so slightly, you lock the arrow between the bow and your hand, resulting in a firm arrow placement.

To begin the draw, place your bow hand out in the direction of your target. Next, begin drawing the string back, with your palm down, using your two fingers to hold your thumb in place around the string.

The Mongolian Draw

Draw the string back until your fist reaches your anchor point. Play with it, as your anchor may be different than mine. I draw till the heel of my palm lines up with the back of my jaw.

Here's the draw from the other side. This motion is much easier on your shoulder, and as a result your shot can be held for a little longer without added discomfort.

SIGNS OF BOW FAILURE AND BOW CARE

A ll bows get old, all bows eventually fail. Whether they are made of wood, horn, fiberglass, carbon fiber, or metal, all bows will fail. This can happen in weeks, it can take centuries, but bows aren't forever. PVC is no exception, and after use it will need to be retired. If not, like any bow, it can break, which can be dangerous like any other bow.

CAUSES OF FAILURE

There are many things that can cause a PVC bow to fail. This can be broken up into three basic reasons. The first is from abrasion or cuts, the second is from UV exposure, and the third is from fatigue. The first two are preventable, the last is inevitable.

ABRASION AND CUTS

This one is fairly straightforward. If an area of the bow that works (flexes during shooting) is abraded too far or is cut, the bow may snap or collapse on that area. The reason this happens is because the bow needs all of its strength in those crucial working areas, and any points of weakness can rapidly spread, causing failure in that area.

The best way to prevent this is to keep the bow from hitting things, and always checking the limbs and handle before stringing and shooting. This can also happen on non-flattened PVC bows if the handle is not protected from the arrow when fired.

UV EXPOSURE

Like most plastics, PVC can be damaged by exposure to UV light. UV light in the form of sunlight, even indirect, can cause many of the compounds that give PVC its flex to leach out of the material. Once this happens, you now have a bow of glass. While it won't happen all of a sudden, UV exposure can cause the bow to collapse even after only an hour or so of sunlight. UV exposure is also especially bad if a bow is left outdoors for a long time and then used.

A bow kept outside for a long time can become so brittle that it may actually blow up when strung, drawn, or shot. The bow becomes like glass and can shatter, sending razor sharp shards of plastic everywhere. These can cut, and in extreme cases can even get embedded into the skin causing pain and open up the possibility of infection. While this in itself may make the idea of a PVC bow sound like a terrible idea, I will say that a fiberglass bow treated the same way can also explode in a similar (often more devastating) manner.

The best way to prevent this is to keep the bow out of direct sunlight for any period longer than an hour or two. If out at the range, keep it covered in a case or under a UV resistant sunshade or black cloth. Another way to help lessen the effects of UV damage is to cover the bow with a UV resistant material. Most duct tapes, leather, heavy cloth, etc. will help keep UV rays from reaching the plastic. Even spray paint can help cut down on UV damage. Also, building your bow from gray PVC conduit will help lessen the effect of UV rays, as this type of PVC has additives in it that help resist UV.

FATIGUE

PVC is a plastic, and part of being a plastic is that it deforms and can lose its shape. Over time, especially if the plastic is under stress or constant flexing, it will deteriorate. Basically the plastic will become tired and will actually stretch easier. In a bow, the first signs will be a drop in draw weight. A bow will also seem more flexible or easier to pull over time.

As long as the bow is well cared for, fatigue is not a big problem. Usually, a bow that is old and heavily fatigued will display some big warning signs before breaking. Even so, a fatigued bow that has not become brittle from UV exposure is far less likely to snap or shatter, and much more likely to simply collapse or develop a large bend. Really, a well-kept bow can last

THE IMPOSSIBLE BOW

a very long time, usually dropping a few pounds before failing, though most bows will give clear indication before failing if they are kept well.

Like I said before, fatigue is not something that can be avoided, it is inevitable. That said, there are some things that can be done to slow down the progression of fatigue. PVC is affected by heat, and the more it is heated up and cooled, the faster it will fatigue. Keep this in mind when making the bow, as too many re-heats will lower the bow's lifespan.

Leaving a bow in a hot car in the sun is also a bad idea, as a deformed bow will need to be re-shaped, and a simply heated bow will fatigue faster. It is also a good idea to unstring the bow after every use. Another thing to keep in mind is that once the bow has been drawn to a set draw length consistently, going beyond that will speed up fatigue as well.

WARNING SIGNS

Very rarely will a bow break without any warning whatsoever. Almost all the time, there will be a sign that the bow is either nearing the end of its life or it is about to break, and should not be ignored. There are six main signs. The first is visible cracking, the second is visible compression fractures, the third is twisting, the fourth is ticking, the fifth is uneven flex, and the sixth is weight loss.

VISIBLE CRACKING

Sometimes small cracks can form on the PVC. They can be hard to see, especially when the bow is unstrung, or if the bow is covered. This is a sign of UV damage, and usually only happens on bows that are not covered, or left out in the sun. This is a sign that the bow may soon snap or shatter, and it may or may not be accompanied by a ticking noise when the bow is drawn. If you notice any visible cracking on a bow, retire it immediately and make another one.

COMPRESSION FRACTURES

Sometimes, the bow will begin to fail on the belly side.

When this happens, the bow will start to form strange waves in its surface. This is usually a sign that the bow is over-stressed in an area and may soon collapse. It may also be a sign of bad bending or tillering, as bending PVC while it is not fully soft can result in a rippled surface.

If you find compression fractures on a tillered bow like the Banded Krait or Indigo Serpent, they can usually be re-heated and re-tillered to compensate for the fracture. Just make sure to thicken those areas so that they don't bend as much. If a compression fracture shows up on a simply bent PVC bow, retire it immediately and build another one.

Twisting

While not a big problem on the tillered bows, the full PVC bows may twist over time. This is because the round pipe likes to bend along the direction of least resistance, and sometimes this means it will bend off to one side. You will start to notice this if you look down the bow from one tip to the other when it is strung. If you notice the bow is starting to twist, simply heat it up and straighten it out. If left unchecked, the bow could simply fold sideways. This may or may not cause a breakage or collapse, but may be irreparable once it happens.

Ticking

While not extremely common, a bow that is brittle through UV damage may make ticking or snapping sounds when it is strung or drawn. If you hear any odd noises when a bow is being strung or drawn, stop drawing the bow. Give it a little test flex away from your body and face, and see if you hear it again. If the bow is still making noise, retire it immediately and make a new one. Even if the bow doesn't tick anymore, it is better to be safe than sorry.

Uneven Flex

If a bow is starting to fatigue, you may notice that one limb starts taking a bend more than the other one, causing the bow to become lopsided. This means that one limb, the limb with the more severe bend, is too weak. One way to fix this is either to thicken up that spot if dealing with a tillered bow, or simply flip the bow over if using a simple PVC bow. If left unchecked, this can result in limb collapse.

Weight Loss

One of the telltale signs of bow fatigue is weight loss. As the plastic begins to fatigue, it will slowly lose weight over time. This is something that should be monitored. If the drop in weight suddenly increases, the bow may be close to collapsing. If the bow also shows other signs, retire it. While fatigue is serious, a well kept bow can sometimes lose as much as thirty pounds before it fails, while some bows may hardly lose any weight at all.

General Care and Average Lifespan

With good care and periodic use, your PVC bow will last for about a year or so. Much like wooden bows, this span can change dramatically. Depending on how it is used, how often it is used, how well it is maintained, etc., the bow can last days or a few years. Bow maintenance is very important. Treating these bows like real bows, and giving them the respect they deserve will allow them to give you many years of service. Treating them like cheap plastic toys will usually cause them to break quickly, like cheap plastic toys.

Caring for Your Bow

Once you have your bow, the first thing you want to do is protect it from the elements. Covering the bow itself or even painting it will help keep it from being heavily affected by sunlight, which is the big threat for a PVC bow. When storing your bow, you want to keep it out of sunlight, even though most window glass filters out UV light.

When storing your bow, you want to keep it in a cool, dark place. You also want to keep the bow horizontal, as storing it on one tip will actually cause one limb to fatigue faster than the other, causing uneven bending. A bow rack or a bow case makes storing your bow easier, but if you have a bed or long closet, just lay the bow flat on the ground in the dark.

When stringing your bow, don't simply push down on the bow, smashing the limbs inwards to string the bow. That's the temptation, but it will cause problems over time like twisting and bow collapse. Most bow stringers won't work on the bows in this bow, so bending the bow with your leg like the first section in this chapter is a good way to go. Once you are done shooting, unstring the bow, especially before it goes into storage or into a car.

When shooting, be sure that your arrow is lined up in the same place on the bow and string. This will keep you from pulling the bow unevenly, which can cause the bow to bend unevenly. It is also a good idea to not draw the bow without an arrow on the string, and make sure you don't point a loaded bow at anything you don't want to shoot.

Firing the bow without an arrow is called dry firing. Now most bows aside from the more modern or bows will break after even one dry firing. To have a bow survive a full dry fire is pure luck, as the energy that normally goes into the arrow feeds back into the bow causing a great deal of stress that can equal failure. A well made PVC bow, on the other hand, can survive the stress of being dry fired occasionally. Now, I am not saying to dry fire your bow, because anything can happen, but all of the many bows I have made of PVC have survived a few test dry-fires without any problems.

Taking care of your bowstring is very important, as a string breaking during use can be very dangerous. The bow whipping back from the release and the string whipping around can all combine to cause injury. Always check your bowstring before shooting and make sure that it isn't fraying or breaking. If it is wearing down, replace it, and if you are using a traditional bowstring, be sure to wax it regularly.

LIFE SPAN

There are so many variables to consider when coming up with even a rough life span for a bow. The way it was made, the state of the materials before the bow was made, how it is cared for, etc.. All of these things add up, making it very hard to pinpoint an actual lifespan. Yet, through all of my experience with PVC bows, I will say that any of these bows should survive at least one year or five hundred shots, assuming that they are well taken care of and shot with respect.

My oldest PVC bow is a seventy pound recurve in the style of the Desert Serpent, except in 1 inch pipe. It was shot at least a hundred times before I decided to put a leather arrow rest on it, it has been painted black, sanded clean, painted again, wrapped with cotton twine, and it has had three strings broken over its lifespan. Now it has fatigued a little and is only sixty pounds at full draw, but beyond that, it is still as dependable as the first day I made it. I have put at least five thousand arrows through it, and it is still going strong.

I have seen similar results with all the other bows I have made, and can say that as long as they are made with care and maintained well, my results can be typical for PVC bows. With that said, enjoy your bow, and may your arrows fly true.

Gallery

A longer version of the Banded Krait, sixty-three inches long. It's a good length for target shooting, and at forty pounds packs a punch. At this length it is pretty fast and quite snappy.

My friend, Nick, trying out his new sixty inch, forty five pound PVC recurve. It's basically just a longer version of the banded krait, which is a very versatile design. Nora looks on as he holds the bow at full draw in the kitchen.

THE IMPOSSIBLE BOW

Here we have my favorite fishing bow. It is in the style of the desert serpent, yet reflexed more in the handle. It's a hard to draw sixty pounds, but it drives an arrow hard into water. It has taken a few large manini (convict tang). It is painted black with a leather arrow pass.

It's the banded krait! Luckily I was using a tripod, and no camerapeople were shot in the taking of this picture.

NICHOLAS TOMIHAMA

Here we have C. Grey Wolf, current Khan of the Khanate of the Golden Horde, a living history society and medieval combat group here in Hawaii. Here he is in armor and holding a forest cobra that has been padded with cardboard and wrapped in duct tape.

The indigo serpent is by far the most bow-like PVC bow I've ever made. Here is actually a different bow than the one in this book. It pulls forty pounds, the extra weight coming from the limbs, which were left thicker than normal.

The Impossible Bow

This is my oldest surviving PVC bow, made in the style of the desert serpent, except scaled up using a five foot long, 1″ ID pipe. It is now only sixty pounds, but here Justin from the Golden Horde is pulling it back to thirty two inches, which brings it back to its old seventy pound weight.

Not sure why I have such a strange expression on my face. It could be a nod to my Asian heritage. Or it could be there was a mosquito near my head. It could also be me wondering if I am going to hit the ceiling of my carport. The world may never know.

Here is Wolf again, in armor, shooting the indigo serpent. The backdrop is one of the cliff-like walls of the park where the Khanate of the Golden Horde meets and practices every week.

Here I am in armor, holding the indigo serpent at a full thirty two inch draw. This is a great illustration of how the limbs bend smoothly, each one a smooth arc, each limb almost coming inward. This is by far my favorite PVC bow as far as its ability to replicate "real bows" goes.

The Impossible Bow

Wolf demonstrating why you should never point a bow or shoot at other people. Things like this could happen. Be safe and don't shoot at people or in the direction of people, no matter how far away or protected they are.

An older picture of one of my early experiments with PVC. This bow is similar in style to the forest cobra, but the nocks are on the ends rather than on the back of the bow. The string had a tendency to slip off the bow at full draw. This picture was taken at the Kapiolani archery range.

Just a little picture of me flattening a bow limb in the kitchen. The four foot board gives just the right amount of angle so that when you stand right in the middle, you get the perfect amount of taper from handle to tip.

A replica of one of my earliest attempts at making a PVC bow. If you skip ahead to the, Ye Olde Stick Flinger section after the glossary and reflections, you'll find out how to make your own. It's a super simple lightweight bow. It's great for kids getting started with archery.

Glossary

Anchor Point - There are two types of anchor points, fixed and floating. An anchor point is basically where the arrow is drawn to during the draw, and where the string and arrow rest just before the arrow is released. Fixed anchors are most common, as they give an easy way to ensure the same shot every time. These are usually at the chin, against the nose, along the jaw, etc.. Floating anchors are anchor points that float in space, usually for bows with a short draw (the anchor is in front of the archer) or an extended draw (the anchor is behind the archer). Both work fine, though the fixed anchor is much easier to get accustomed to.

Arm Guard - An arm guard is a device that protects the arm from the string hitting the arm when the string is released. This can be a simple pad that protects the arm, a rigid surface over the inside of the wrist, or even a full bracer which covers the entire inner forearm.

Arrow - A projectile that is fired from a bow. An arrow usually consists of a nock or nocking point, fletchings or vanes to stabilize the arrow in flight, a shaft which is the main bulk of the arrow and to which all the other parts are attached to or carved out of, and a point or tip. The arrow shaft may be constructed of wood, cane, fiberglass, aluminum, and carbon fiber. For bows that are shot off the hand, wood and aluminum are good choices as they are less likely to cause injury, and work well in slower bows. Aluminum arrows are the best for shooting off the hand in regards to longevity, straightness, ease of tuning, and safety. Arrows may have vanes or feather fletchings to stabilize the arrow in flight, and for the bows in this book, feathers are best as they fold down as opposed to plastic vanes which do not.

Arrow Pass - The area where the arrow passes over when the bow is drawn and shot. This area can be unmarked, marked, reinforced with another material, or even part of an arrow rest.

Arrow Rest - A shelf or raised area on a bow that allows the arrow to literally rest on during the draw and while being shot. An arrow rest also gives a constant placement for the arrow, eliminating one more variable when learning to shoot.

Asiatic Composite Bow - Style of bow which usually uses sinew and horn laminated to a wood core. These bows are usually shorter than their selfbow equivalents and are often faster due to the nature of the materials used and their design. Bows of this type are fairly easily to replicate in shape with PVC pipe.

Brace - The distance between the back of the bow's handle and string when the bow is strung up.

Centershot - A style of bow that allows the arrow to rest center, aligned with the string. With this style of bow, the effects of archer's paradox are lessened, as the arrow does not have to flex around the handle as in a non centershot bow.

Composite Bow - A composite bow is any bow that is made up of more than one material that is attached by gluing (lamination) or binding on the working parts of the bow. This can range from a bow that simply has a backing or siyah glued on, to a bow that is composed of many layers of different materials, all laminated together.

Compression - It is the force that the belly of a flexed bow undergoes. Compression is a pushing force, meaning that the object being compressed is basically being pushed into itself. Compression can cause a permanent reduction in volume in the object being compressed, which is half of the reason why a new bow will change its shape with use, bending toward the side of the bow that is under compression.

Deflex - Any curve in a bow's limbs or handle that bend towards the archer. The Banded Krait has a deflex in the handle area.

The Impossible Bow

Draw - To draw the bow is to pull back on the string, in preparation to fire the bow.

Draw Force - The amount of force required to pull a bow to its full draw. This is often considered the basis for a bow's strength, and is most often rated in pounds, as draw weight.

Draw Length - The length of your draw. Depending on how long your arms are and where you feel comfortable drawing to, your draw may be above, below, or at twenty eight inches. Twenty eight inches is more or less of a standard, but draw lengths can range from well below twenty four inches, and well above thirty eight inches.

Draw Weight - The amount or weight equivalent it takes to pull a bow to full draw. In most places, draw weight is measured at 28 inches, which is considered the standard full draw (though draw lengths vary from under twenty four to over thirty four inches). Draw weight is often used to measure the potential attributes of a bow, and is used by states to determine the minimum strength of a bow for hunting, or by archery combat organizations to determine a maximum strength for shooting at people. Draw weight can be easily determined with a pull-scale, or by hanging weights off of a bow string where the arrow should rest. For example, a fifty pound bow with a fifty pound weight attached to it, should flex all the way to its full draw when the weight is applied.

Duct Tape - An adhesive backed cloth reinforced plastic tape that is commonly used for watertight repairs. It is used for just about everything nowadays for repairs, decoration, and crafts. It comes in many different colors, adhesive strengths, thicknesses, and UV resistance.

Electrical Tape - A flexible vinyl adhesive-backed tape that is often used in electrical work due to its good properties as an electric insulator. It is quite stretchy, and can fade and turn brittle with time and exposure to sunlight. It can come in many different colors, but is most commonly black.

Fades - The fades, or the fade-outs, are the area where the handle transitions to the limbs. On most bows, this area is characterized by either a flattening or a widening. On some bows, there are no fades, as the bow's handle is part of the working limbs.

Fistmele - One way to measure brace. To find this height make a fist, then a thumb's up. Place your fist on the handle of the bow, and the string should reach the tip of your thumb at full brace. This is usually around six inches or so.

Full Brace - When a bow is strung up to its full distance between the string and handle. Full brace can vary anywhere from four to ten inches. The lower the brace, the easier it usually is on the bow, and the quieter the bow when fired. The higher the brace, the harder it is on the bow and the louder the sound of the string, as much of the bow's energy feeds back into the bow when fired at a high brace.

Full Draw - When the bow is pulled to the full length it was designed for. Full draw varies depending on the bow.

Half Brace - When a bow is strung up with the a longer string, making the distance between the handle and the string around half of the bow's full brace.

Inside Diameter - When dealing with PVC pipe, the measure of a pipe is given in its inside diameter or ID. This is measured across the inside of the pipe. For example, a 1″ Schedule 40 pipe is actually approximately one inch in diameter on the inside, while on the outside it is closer to one and a quarter inches.

LARP - Live Action Role Play is a type of recreational activity that is based upon the early turn-based fantasy role playing games and modern computer-based role playing games. In LARP, players create a persona or character and then pick a class, which determines the type of weapons and other attributes of your character. LARP's combat system is based mostly on minimal or no contact, and bows used in LARP archery combat need to be on the weaker side to be considered safe to use. PVC bows are great for this sort of combat as they can be made to fit almost any shape, and can be made to pull light weights as well.

The Impossible Bow

Long Bow - A long bow is typically a bow with straight limbs though this is not always the case. The bow may have reflex and deflex, but usually the tips are left either straight, lightly reflexed, or deflexed.

Mediterranean Draw - Another name for the three finger release and draw. It was common in Europe, and is the most popular draw and release used today. It has become the standard for modern archery, supplanted only by mechanical releases.

Medieval Reenactment - A type of recreational activity which is based on promoting awareness of the history of the Middle Ages through art, crafts, medieval combat, and re-creating life as it may have been back then. Many groups encourage participants to create a name and persona in order to re-enact medieval life. Since archery played a pivotal role in medieval Europe and Asia, archery and bow-making is often practiced by many groups. The PVC bow offers the ability to make a period-correct bow that is low-cost.

Mongolian Draw/Release - Another name for the thumb draw, named for the Mongols who used the thumb draw extensively. It is also known as the thumb draw or the Turkish release, as the Turks also used the thumb draw and short composite bow to great effect.

Nock - A nock is where the string rests either on a bow or on an arrow. On a bow, the string nocks are located on the top and bottom tips of the bow, and hold the string in place when the bow it at brace. The nocks also hold onto the string while the bow is drawn and shot. On an arrow the string nock is the slot at the back of the arrow that the string is inserted to secure the arrow to the string.

Off the Hand - A style shooting a bow in which no rest or shelf holds the arrow up. The arrow rests off the first knuckle or the thumb of the bow-holding hand. Many bows of traditional cultures are shot in this way.

Overdraw - When a bow is drawn further than it was intended, it has been overdrawn. An overdraw may also refer to any draw that is longer than twenty eight inches. Mostly, overdrawing a bow past its safe draw length is dangerous. Since the bow is being drawn further than it is designed for, the bow may break or collapse. Another danger to overdrawing is the danger of the arrow falling off of the bow rest and being driven into your hand or arm when the bow is released.

Primary Release - The most basic or the methods to draw and release a bow. It is performed by simply pinching the bow string and arrow between the thumb and forefinger. It is the draw most people commonly use if they have never before used a bow. Common among many cultures, the primary release or pinch release, is best suited for weaker bows or bows that are drawn a short distance. It works very well with snap shooting, as the action of the string simply slipping from the pinch grip results in the arrow being released cleanly. The arrow can rest on either side of the bow.

PVC - Polyvinyl Chloride is a thermoplastic polymer that is used for many different applications. Like most synthetic polymers, it can be damaged by exposure to UV light. It can be softened and shaped with heat, which does make it vulnerable to become soft when exposed to heat. PVC is used in a variety of applications that usually play to its non-conductivity, resistance to corrosion, and its water resistance.

PVC Conduit - PVC pipe made as a non-metal alternative to metallic pipes used to house electrical wiring. It is non-conductive and contains stabilizers which make it resistant to UV damage. This makes it ideal for use in PVC bows, though it also contains softeners which lower its speed and draw force. The trade off here is increased durability and safety at a loss of performance and power.

PVC Plumbing Pipe - Pipe made of PVC, used commonly for waste water and cold water transportation. It is used because it does not corrode like metal pipes and is easier to work with as it can be sealed and fused to other PVC pipe with adhesives. This pipe is usually white or light gray and comes in different schedules. The thinner pipes are for cold water, commonly for sprinkler systems, and the thicker pipes can be used for warm water, sewage, and for structural applications. It is vulnerable to UV light.

Recurve Bow - A bow with tips that are recurved, meaning that the tips bend away from the archer, sometimes abruptly. These bows generally faster than similarly designed straight bows.

Reflex - Any curve in a bow's limbs or handle that bend away from the archer. The handle of the Indigo Serpent is reflexed.

Release - The release is the action of letting go of the arrow and bowstring at full draw to fire a bow. Release can also refer to the style of release used, whether it be primary, secondary, tertiary, three finger, or thumb.

Release Aid - Anything that assists the archer in drawing and releasing the string while shooting a bow. This can range from a glove to protect the fingers, to thumb rings, to mechanical releases and trigger releases which hold the string in place until the release is opened.

Riser - A riser is the entire handle section of a bow. This area includes the hand grip, the arrow pass, any arrow rests, and is usually separated from the limbs by an area known as the fades.

Schedule - A method of standardizing plastic pipe. Schedule refers to the pipe wall thickness. For example, all schedule 40 pipe has the same wall thickness, regardless of inside diameter. SDR, on the other hand, is based on pressure ratings, so that the larger the inside diameter, the thicker the wall thickness.

Secondary Release - Much like the primary release, the secondary release consists of the string and arrow being pinched between thumb and forefinger. To allow greater strength in the draw and control, the middle finger also rests on the string, assisting the thumb and forefinger by taking some of the pressure from the string. Like the primary release, the arrow may rest on either side of the bow.

Serving - A wrapping or binding on a string along the points of contact to ensure a longer string life. There are two basic types of serving. The first, also called the center serving, goes over the nocking area of the arrow. This helps prevent the arrow nock from abrading and weakening the string, and it also thickens the string, allowing the arrow's nock to fit better. The second type of serving is used to pad the top and bottom loops of the string. This not only cuts down on the string rubbing against the bow and fraying, but it can also protect the nocks of your bow from being cut into by a small string. A center serving should be applied on any string, though only continuous loop strings need end servings (though it can be applied to counter-twist and braided strings).

Siyah - A raised tip on Asiatic composite bows. It acts like a lever, and is a type of static recurve. They are usually thicker than they are wide, and may or may not have a groove on the belly side for the string to sit.

Snap Shot - A type of shooting in which you aim at a target, draw back quickly, then release the arrow once the resistance of the string forces you to release. This style of release allows a clean release, and is well suited for bows that have short draw lengths. The bow is simply drawn to the maximum draw length and released. This works well with a floating anchor point.

Stack - Stack or stacking occurs when a bow's weight rapidly increases per inch of draw. This is an indication of either the bow being drawn farther than its design can compensate for, or the material it is made of being too stiff to pull further comfortably. Stack is the reason why the simple bent PVC bows are very light, then build up rapidly and stiffly to their full weight.

Static Handle - Any handle section that does not bend when the bow is at full draw. The Indigo Serpent and Banded Krait are good examples of static handles.

The Impossible Bow

Static Recurve - Any bow with recurved tips that do not bend during the draw. These tips act like levers, not unfurling during the draw.

String - The string is the long cord that runs from one nock of the bow to the other, and holds the bow under tension when the bow is strung. The bow string allows the archer to flex the limbs of the bow, and it also propels the arrow during the shot. Strings can be made of various fibers, whether they be animal, plant, or synthetic. Silk and sinew are animal fibers most often used for strings, hemp and linen (flax) are plant fibers often used, and Dacron (polyester) is a synthetic string material often used. There are other fibers that may be used, though Dacron is one the most reliable for the bows in this book. Strings may also be continuous loop, meaning they are composed of a single strand of string material looped around a number of times. They can be twisted or braided, meaning a number of different strands are twisted or braided together and the ends spliced into loops.

String Bridge - A raised pad on the belly side of a bow that the string rests on while the bow is braced. The string bridge also helps hold the string in place during the early part of the draw, and usually has a place for the string to track when the bow is fired. They are common on many types of Asiatic composite bows.

Tension - It is the force that the back of a flexed bow undergoes. Tension is a pulling, force, meaning that the object under tension is being pulled on. Tension can cause a permanent increase in volume in the object under tension, which is half of the reason why a new bow will change its shape with use, bending away from the side of the bow under tension.

Tertiary Release - Like the primary and secondary releases, the tertiary release uses the thumb and forefinger to hold the arrow in place while the bow is drawn. The middle and ring fingers are placed on the string below the pinch draw to allow for less finger strain and more control. The arrow may be placed on either side of the bow.

Three Finger Release - A type of draw and release that makes use of the first, middle, and ring fingers. This style of release allows even heavy bows to be drawn with minimal pressure on the drawing hand as only the finger tips grip the string. This also results in a fairly easy release, as the string needs to only slip past the three fingers. Because of the torque on the string during the release and the way the string rolls off the fingers, the arrow should be placed on the inside of the bow, facing your bow holding arm. The arrow can be placed either between the first and middle fingers with one over two under (split fingers), or with all three fingers below (three under). The second method of drawing allows you to sight down the arrow shaft as it brings the arrow closer to your eye.

Thumb Release - A type of draw and release that mainly uses the thumb to grip the string. The thumb wraps over the string and the first and middle fingers usually wrap around the thumb, holding it in place. The thumb acts as a lever, holing the string and arrow in place until the fingers release, causing the thumb to move out of the way, much like some mechanical releases. This release is good for short bows that have a high string angle, as it lessens the effect of string pinch. Because of the motion of the string as it rolls off of the thumb, the arrow should be placed on the outside of the bow, away from the bow holding arm.

Thumb Ring - A ring that is worn on the thumb that protects the thumb from the strain of holding the weight of a drawn bow when using a thumb draw. They can be made of a variety of materials, but should at the very least give a place for the string to rest during the draw, and protect some part of the thumb during the shot. It is a type of release aid.

Tiller - A device used by bowyers to view the flex a bow is under from a safe distance. To tiller a bow is to adjust its bending so that the bow is at its most efficient flex. Tillering is the act of using a tiller to adjust the flex of a bow, and a tillered bow is one that has an evenly distributed flex.

The Impossible Bow

UV Light - Light that is just outside the visible spectrum, called ultraviolet because it closest in wavelength to the color violet in the visible light spectrum. It is emitted by the sun and many types of electrical lighting. It can cause synthetic polymers to deteriorate and degrade, causing then to discolor, fade, crack, or completely disintegrate depending on the amount of exposure. Some types of PVC pipe have UV inhibitors in them, and are often gray in color.

Vinyl - Vinyl is the common name for many products made of PVC. It is often flexible and used in many applications where its water resistance is prized. Vinyl is often used as artificial leather in upholstery, as shelf liners, and for waterproof clothing.

Nicholas Tomihama
Acknowledgements

I would like to thank everyone who was involved with this work, and those who inspired me to even consider this in the first place. I would like to first take the time to give thanks to a very good friend of mine who was there from the very beginnings of this book, and who gave me the motivation and drive to finish it. This has not been an easy work, and much of my better judgement and sense of pride as a bowyer have prevented me from completing it many a time.

I would like to dedicate this book to a good friend who I've known for almost half of my life, a friend who has been an inspiration, a wealth of knowledge, an ear to listen, a shoulder to cry on, and above all someone on whom I could always depend. He was the first one to consider my talents when nobody believed I could ever write a book, the first owner of my first book, and the support I needed to write many more.

I dedicate this book to Christopher Yasuhide Okamura, a true friend and the reason behind the whole book. He believed when others didn't, always supporting me to think beyond what is accepted. He was influential in my development of PVC pipe bows, and the reason why I sought out Grey Wolf, Khan of the Khanate of the Golden Horde, in the first place. If not for him, this book would not exist.

His passing has had a profound effect on my life in as many ways as his life did. This book, which almost was abandoned twice, had been rekindled once by his life, and once more by his death. He had always told me to not give up and that I needed to keep going. This book has been more complex and contains more information than I thought would be possible for this topic. Yasuhide, I will always remember you and the good time we shared, and you will always by Uncle Octopus to me and my son, your Godson.

THE IMPOSSIBLE BOW

I would also like to thank my wife, who has always been by my side and stuck by me when I was doing strange things with plastic pipe in the kitchen. She has been a guiding light in many ways, and has pushed me when I could go no further. I commend her for spending many days alone while I flung arrows in the carport or burned my hands on molten plastic. I could not ask for a more supportive and understanding wife.

Thanks also to Grey Wolf and the Khanate of the Golden Horde for giving me an opportunity to explore and develop these PVC bows, and the opportunity to shoot them at people (in armor, of course). Special thanks goes out to Justin and Wolf, who both allowed me to put their pictures in this book. I would also like to thank Wolf for being a sounding board for my ideas, allowing me to develop them, and for making an appearance on the book's cover in full armor.

And last but certainly not least, I want to thank you. Thank you so much for taking the time to read this book and what it has to offer. I hope that it has been worthwhile to you and hope you enjoy your new bow (or bows). If it wasn't for you, none of this would be worth anything at all, so thanks again! So what are you still doing here? Go out there and get shooting!

Nicholas Tomihama

Ye Olde Stick Flinger

(Bonus Track)

As I said in the introduction, one of my first bows was a 1/2″ PVC pipe with some twine for a string. Well, I also mentioned another bow, made in a similar fashion. The stick flinger, remember? Yeah, that's the one! Well, I figure since I've written a book on PVC bows, it would be an embarrassment to skip out on the simplest way to make one. Like I've said before, it has its downsides, but it makes a fun stick flinger and a great little bow for kids and kids at heart.

Like I said before, it doesn't really feel right, nor does it look right as far as bows are concerned. It's light weight, only about twenty pounds at twenty eight inches (10#@20″, 15#@24″, 20#@28″, 30#@32″), but it flings sticks and arrows very well, I must say! This isn't the best bow in the book, but it is the easiest to make. In fact, this particular one took only five minutes, string included!

Like my early attempt at a PVC bow, this one is a five foot piece of 3/4″ schedule 40 pipe with simple nocks. It uses 1/8″ braided nylon rope that can be found at any hardware store for a string, and can be used with arrows, or even plain ole sticks! This design is really simple, and since I first made mine, I've seen tons of these in the hands of kids and adults alike! I bet you or someone you know has already made one of these puppies before. If I win, read the chapter anyway. If I lose, then I'll show you how to make your very own Stick Flinger! Read on!

Start with a five foot long 3/4" PVC pipe.

Cut a 1/4" deep nock half an inch in from the end.

The Impossible Bow

Repeat on the other limb, making sure they line up.

To make a simple string, all you need is a length of rope. Braided nylon rope in 1/8″ or 3/16″ thickness and at least forty pounds of strength will work. These can be found in virtually any hardware store.

Take the end of your rope like this.

Bring the end of the rope behind, forming a loop.

The Impossible Bow

Fold the end of the rope around, bringing it around the other side of the loop.

Tuck the end into the loop.

Wind the end of the rope around the inside of the loop like this.

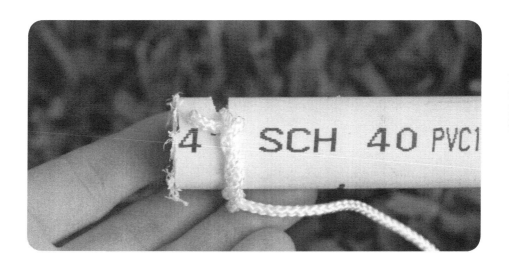

Slip it over the nock end of the pipe.

THE IMPOSSIBLE BOW

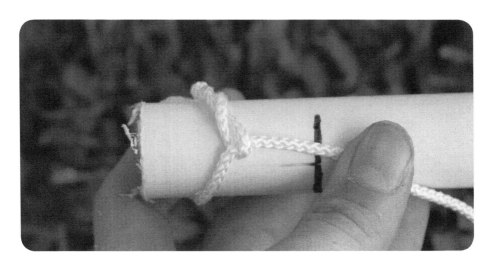

Pull on the rope hard in a side to side motion to lock the knot in place.

Cut the rope so that it ends up just a bit longer than your pipe.

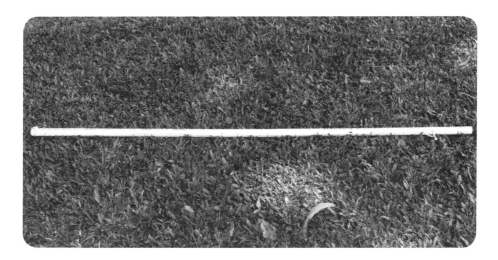

Tie another loop on the other side of the string. This loop should end up five to six inches short of the other nock.

String the bow up like in the caring for your bow section.

The Impossible Bow

Here it is at a seven inch brace.

And here it is at full draw! Enjoy your new stick flinger!

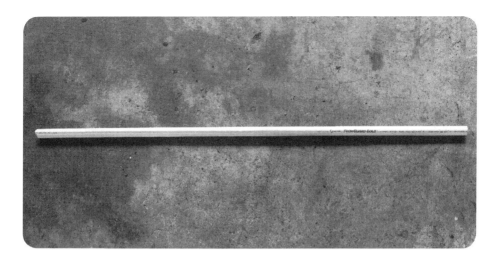

In the spirit of PVC, one type of stick that is fun to fling around is a 1/2" CPVC pipe. These are the very small, thin walled PVC pipes found in the plumbing section of most home improvement stores.

This can also be done with wooden dowels, just be sure the dowels have straight grain. If you want to make arrows out of dowel, check out my other book. The information for it can be found after this chapter, at the end of the book.

THE IMPOSSIBLE BOW

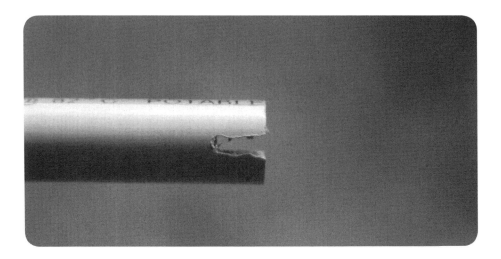

Simply cut a notch a little smaller than the diameter of your string, at least 1/4" deep.

And there you go! You can also fling any stick or rod-like object if you use a pinch grip. Have fun! If this is your first bow, go ahead to the front of the book and try some of the others out!

About the Author

Nicholas Tomihama has written five books which focus on his passion of working with his hands, a passion that has stuck with him since childhood. The son of an award winning jeweler, Nicholas has spent much of his young life experimenting with countless crafts and hobbies.

As a writer, Nicholas focuses on teaching others many of the things he has taught himself over the years. Currently residing in Honolulu, Hawaii with his wife Angela and son Levi, Nicholas spends much of his time building fine wooden bows and arrows. He is a full-time author and writer, as well as an avid archer and hunter who enjoys spending time out in nature with his family.

More Books by the Author

For anyone interested in building a wooden bow, <u>The Backyard Bowyer</u> is the perfect first step. With over 300 photographs and detailed descriptions, <u>The Backyard Bowyer</u> will show you how to build your very first wooden bow with simple hand tools. No shop or previous experience is required to build your own simple target flat bow, an English style longbow, and even a string and arrows to go with them.

-Paperback, Black and White
-194 Pages

Anyone who is involved with archery knows that you can never have enough arrows. As an arrow material, wooden dowels have been prized ever since the early days of modern archery in the early 1900's. Since then, quality has gone down, but fine arrow shafts still remain among the mass-produced dowels. <u>The Dowel Arrow Handbook</u> is a resource for finding suitable dowels and crafting your own quality arrows for target archery and hunting.

-Paperback, Black and White
-96 Pages

Made in the USA
San Bernardino, CA
23 March 2014